TWENTY-EIGHT

TWENTY-EIGHT

*Stories from the
Section 28 Generation*

Reconnecting Rainbows Press

EDITED AND CURATED BY

Kestral Gaian

WITH CONTRIBUTIONS FROM

Chris-Jae Angel, Eric Banks, Claire Beveridge, Ash Brockwell,
James Corley, Kestral Gaian, Kit Gee, Phoebe Green, Quenby
Harley, Dalton Harrison, Harris Eddie Hill, Alex Hilton, Harvey
Humphrey, Owen J Hurcum, Sarah Jones, Bryony Joy Kirkpatrick,
Elise Lennox, Len Lukowski, Colin Mackay, Carrie Marshall,
Mandy McMillan, John Naples-Campbell, George Parker, Ely
Percy, Elaine Scattermoon, Jaime Starr, Oliver Starr, Quen Took,
Jamie Wareham, Beth Watson

CONTENTS

Edited and curated by **Kestral Gaian**

Contributions by: Chris-Jae Angel, Eric Banks, Claire Beveridge, Ash Brockwell, James Corley, Kestral Gaian, Kit Gee, Phoebe Green, Quenby Harley, Dalton Harrison, Harris Eddie Hill, Alex Hilton, Harvey Humphrey, Owen J Hurcum, Sarah Jones, Bryony Joy Kirkpatrick, Elise Lennox, Len Lukowski, Colin Mackay, Carrie Marshall, Mandy McMillan, John Naples-Campbell, George Parker, Ely Percy, Elaine Scattermoon, Jaime Starr, Oliver Starr, Quen Took, Jamie Wareham, Beth Watson

First Edition, *1st February 2023*

The author of this book would like to express a formal dislike of Margaret Thatcher.

Reconnecting Rainbows Press CIC (14570208) is a community interest company registered in the United Kingdom. All of our profits go back into helping marginalised communities publish their works and tell their stories.

www.reconnectingrainbows.co.uk

NOTES FROM THE EDITOR

Queerphobia is not a new phenomenon. Nor is queer love and acceptance. From the celebration of trans identities in Ancient Greece through to the puritanical movements of the 15th century, the LGBTQIA+ community has see-sawed through history being loved and reviled in equal measure.

The 20th Century was no stranger to this turmoil. The early 1900s saw the first documented gay marriage, but also a spate of laws designed to criminalise homosexual conduct and make things like gay marriage explicitly illegal. The extreme politics and policies of two world wars devastated queer folk who had been living comfortable-if-quiet lives across Europe, and put in motion a series of moral panics that came to a head in the late 60s. Stonewall was no accident.

The fight for queer rights was heating up and grabbing headlines - but in 1981 something new came along to eclipse the progress that was being made. Known at first as 'Gay Pneumonia' then KS, GRID, and eventually AIDS, this epidemic presented queer detractors with a chance to paint LGBTQIA+ people as dangerous to public health. And, sadly, they did not miss a beat.

Here in the UK, our leaders refused to help those who were suffering and dying. Instead, then-prime-minister Margaret Thatcher declared that a return to "traditional moral values" was what was needed to save us from the "homosexual menace". This was achieved with Section 28 of the Local Government Act 1988.

"A local authority shall not intentionally promote homosexuality or publish material with the intention of promoting homosexuality; or promote the teaching in any maintained school of the acceptability of homosexuality as a pretended family relationship."

With those thirty-five words, several generations of young LGBTQIA+ people were effectively damned.

What lies before you in the pages of this book are an antidote to a virus of hate that once filled our homes, schools, and lives. Stories from people like you - and like me - who have been impacted by a law so Machiavellian and vile that its dark legacy is still felt nearly two decades after its repeal.

Like most people who grew up in the shadow of Section 28, it took me a long time to come to terms with how it had impacted me. It's always the way - when something is dark, designed to turn a community against itself, the pain becomes internal. My unconscious bias and internal prejudice against my own community, and against myself, was insidious and hidden for the longest time.

It was through community that I found understanding, strength, and answers to some of the questions that had plagued me for half my life. Why did I hate myself so much? Because I was taught to, by a law and a society that prioritised conformity over individuality. Compliance over comfort. Hate over love.

As adults now we are speaking out. This is the legacy of Section 28.

These are our stories.

* * *

Editing, curating, and contributing to this book has been a privilege. I am immensely proud of the stories that are told here, and it's been one of my greatest pleasures to work with such an incredible range of wonderful contributors.

As you thumb through the pages ahead, I hope you get to feel the same sense of appreciation, solidarity, and gratitude that I have on reading them.

Let's make sure history never repeats itself.

Kestral Gaian

CHAPTER 1

Section 28 and Modern Transphobia

BY OWEN J HURCUM
(THEY/THEM)

Owen J Hurcum came out as non-binary in 2019 and was the first openly non-binary Mayor of any City after becoming Mayor of Bangor in 2021. They are a former editor for LGBTQymru Magazine and author of the book 'Don't Ask About My Genitals'.

Content Warnings
Homophobia, Transphobia, Sex Shaming, 'Social Contagion' Conspiracy, Tories

PREFACE

The modern anti-trans hysteria is a quintessential moral panic, and one that I feel is fuelled both by the ignorance that Section 28 caused the public to have about LGBTQIA+ existence, but also by this current Tory Government's wish to recreate a similar policy as a way to 'resolve' the moral panic they created. This chapter will explore this, as well as discussing what the legacy of Section 28 personally meant to me as I went through my school career.

I was 6 years old when Section 28 was repealed, an age far younger than some other contributors to this book, and one which placed me in year one of the British schooling system. A different situation to other authors, who were subjected to the law throughout their entire student career. Yet as young as I was when Section 28 was repealed, it, and its immediate legacy, still had a significant bearing on me and my journey to understand, accept and love my queer self. Whilst studies have shown that for some members of our LGBTQIA+ community they already knew and are sure of their identity at that age, I however wasn't. Though it is probable that had it not been illegal to have taught me about the existence of our community at that age – I may well have realised back then.

* * *

I would realise my queerness several years later when I was around 12 or 13 years of age. Looking back, I can clearly see the signs from when I was younger than this of me being my true fabulous self, but I say it was the onset of teenagerhood that eradicated any doubt in my mind about myself having a form of queer sexuality in some way. This is because it was at this age, shortly after starting High School, that I got a crush on a classmate who, whilst I was still playing at being a boy, was a guy (it would take me longer to understand and accept my non-binary identity).

This was around 2010, and as mentioned, it was several years after Section 28 had been repealed. Yet despite it no longer being a crime for schools to provide an education that would have delivered much needed information on the LGBTQIA+ community, such an education was depressingly absent even by the time I knew my own Queerness. Indeed, my only 'education' about our community from school up until that point was that being gay was bad, being a lesbian was for sluts, and either way you deserved to be bullied – an 'education' that will be all too familiar to people who went through the British schooling system at a similar time to myself. Those ideas were ingrained into you on the playground by other students, who likewise were clueless to anything genuine about us.

I can't tell you when exactly I learned what the word 'gay' meant in terms of a sexuality, but I can tell you it certainly didn't come from a PCHSE lesson at school. In fact, my earliest recollection of even using that word within the education system (and not as an insult on the playground) was during a year five sex education lesson where I asked if we would learn about 'being gay'. Looking back, it's clear I was asking because I was figuring myself out – though I know I would have asked it in such a way as to make it seem like a joke, so I wouldn't get bullied by my peers for being assumed to be gay. Either way, I can't remember the teacher's exact reply – all I do know is that we weren't taught about it.

I mention all this because I feel this small personal story demonstrates that Section 28 existed in essence long after it had officially been taken off the books, and to provide my personal anecdote of Britain's 'Don't' Say Gay' law before delving into the main topic of my chapter. I survived Section 28. But moreover I survived its immediate legacy that ensured that even though it was removed during my early schooling, I never once got the opportunity to learn about our community during the rest of my primary, middle and high school career. Indeed, it is this legacy of Section 28 that is the focus of this chapter: specifically how Section 28 may well be a main factor in the anti-trans hysteria currently gripping the UK, or, as it is aptly named, TERF Island.

* * *

I don't think many readers will be unaware of this alternative name for these (un)fair Isles. I could probably write an entire book (which I, and many others have) on how we came to be known by that name and so I won't cover everything here in this small section, contained within a single chapter - but for those reading this who may not be so aware, I shall briefly explain some of it.

I do ask the reader to bear in mind, however, that a lot can change regarding our rights as trans people very quickly. Indeed, when I penned the first draft of this chapter during the first 2022 Conservative Leadership Election to decide who our next Prime Minister would be, several of the candidates made promises to make the UK even more hostile to trans people should they win the Premiership. Indeed, one of the more transphobic candidates did win, Liz Truss, who appointed the UK's most anti-LGBTQIA+ cabinet in recent history. Of course, her Premiership lasted only 2.8% as long as the average wait to see a Gender Identity Clinic in the UK (at 42 days) – and now the new PM (if he still is when this is published) is also openly trans-hostile.

Back to my present. Whilst the 2010 Equality Act does recognize being trans as a protected characteristic, and you can theoretically obtain a medical transition through the NHS – the reality is that unless you are willing to wait upwards of around 5 years for a first appointment with a Gender Identity Clinic you won't be going through the NHS (or if you want any of the numerous services they flat out don't provide or have stopped providing). Equally, whilst trans people are legally recognized (for now) here, that doesn't extend to trans people who happen to be non-binary: we are, according to the government, 'too complicated' to recognize. Further, the UK does not allow Self-ID for trans people.

Trans woman are getting banned from competing as women in more and more sports. The ability for trans people to access gendered spaces that match our real gender is constantly under attack, and the notion of a gender-neutral bathroom has become so egregious to some that a law is being penned to stop new public buildings having them. Businesses and our Government are removing themselves from associating with Stonewall (who themselves are now under constant and direct attack), so-called feminists are publicly vilifying those who affirm trans children and well, I could go on but I think the picture is being clearly painted. Being trans right now in the UK is not exactly a stroll in the park.

All this is being driven by - and there really isn't a better way of describing it - the cult of TERFism. This cult being the community of people with anti-trans views coming together to spread disinformation about trans people, and even in extreme cases stripping their own children's rights to free association, based on their bigoted ideology. How is the cult of TERFism doing this, then? How and why is it so influential to the point that it can make transphobia not only an electable position in the UK – but a major talking point for some politicians and parties? Well, the answer, I would argue, can be traced to Section 28.

* * *

As a student of Queer Archaeology, I can categorically state it has not always been like this. The trans community, even here, has not always been the focus of such widespread and public condemnation for just existing. We have burial evidence, in the form of the Harper Road burial, suggesting that trans women were seen accepted as women in Roman London. Further, the UK is home to some of the earliest written records relating to a trans person, that being Eleanor

Rykener in 1395. In more recent times, trans people were able to exist publicly without the same levels of widespread harassment. They were welcomed and celebrated by most in their local communities, such as with Mark and David Furrow of Yarmouth in 1936, Dana International's Eurovision win in 1998, or Nadia Almada's 2004 Big Brother win. This is, of course, not to say it was easy for these or other trans people at the time, and that they didn't face harassment or prejudice - simply that the mass hysteria and frenzy being whipped up into a culture war by our current media and government is more a recent turning point.

The climate for such hostility has occurred, I feel, due to an accidentally perfect combination of trans representation alongside ignorance by those who were educated before, and in particular during, Section 28. Trans representation is nothing new: in films we have been represented since the start, such as in *Meet Me at The Fountain* (1904), we have been featured in early 20th century books both written about us and by us, such as with *Man Into Woman* (1931) or *Autobiography of an Androgyne* (1918) and medical papers frequently discuss 'sexual inverts' (as we were lovingly referred to at the time) from the late 1800s onwards. Yet it cannot be said that this representation was really mainstream, and it would not be until far more recently (thanks to the work of LGBTQIA+ activists) that trans representation would start to not only be more accurate and less hostile, but also more accessible.

This, however, has meant that trans people are starting to get more and more noticed in pieces of media by generations who before could quite easily have lived a life completely ignorant to our existence. If we combine this broader and more accessible representation, accelerated by the internet and social media, with the growing number of people feeling more confident and comfortable being publicly their true trans selves, then conflict with those ignorant of the trans community was unfortunately inevitable.

The ignorance that allows this conflict, and the bigotry of those hostile towards us, can be placed squarely at the feet of Section 28. This legislation, being in place as it was from 1988-2003 in England and Wales (and until 2000 in Scotland), means that anyone born from around 1976 to around 1995 would have had a significant period of their education where they legally could not have been educated about our LGBTQIA+ community, and with many of those (such as myself) who were born after 1995 to more recently partaking in an education system still ill-equipped and unwilling to teach about our community because of how Section 28 had impacted the education system. Indeed, it wouldn't be until 2020 that England would mandate LGBTQIA+ inclusive education in all state schools, both primary and secondary, and in Wales this was due to start in 2022.

All this means that anyone from around their late twenties and older in the UK (at the time of writing this in 2022) was either educated primarily by a system where the teaching of LGBTQIA+ identities and lives was a crime, or who saw Section 28 being implemented first-hand. Those around my age and slightly younger, as explained in the intro to my chapter, are also still being impacted directly by the immediate legacy of Section 28 on the education system.

To put that into perspective, around 80% of the current UK population were alive when Section 28 was on the books. That means around a third of the population completed part of their education under this law. Knowing this, is it any wonder there is still a current of anti-LGBTQIA+ sentiment in the UK, and particularly the rising anti-trans hysteria in the face of our increased representation when we know ignorance breeds bigotry? And yes, people who weren't educated about our community at school aren't inherently bigoted against us, it is just that they are more susceptible to anti-trans arguments because they don't have to challenge anything they learned about us during their formative years.

The rising anti-trans sentiment in the UK owes itself completely to this fact. There is a reason a transphobe's main 'gotcha' goes along the lines of talking about "basic biology" or a simplistic 'understanding' of English grammar. For them, part of their opposition to trans people really does originate from being told at school that there are only two genders, based on binary sex chromosomes. Both of these statements are wrong to begin with.

They have then become unwilling to update their knowledge past that. I'm sure there would be less transphobia and fewer transphobes if the correct science was taught to them during their schooling. Even then, even if still told that incorrect science, I reckon many more would be willing to update their knowledge on trans people today if they had just been told that being gay was fine. This would have allowed them to see the world through less prejudiced eyes, but Section 28 denied that.

I don't just hold Section 28 responsible for creating the environment that has allowed transphobia to flourish in the present, but also, I see it as something that this current government is desperately trying to bring back with a focus on trans people. Section 28, through its ins and outs, was designed explicitly to stop children being gay. Thatcher speaking to the Conservative Party Conference in 1987 said that children are being taught that they "have an inalienable right to be gay" and that that is robbing them of "a sound start in life".

It is, of course, not possible to achieve this as you cannot legislate out a characteristic that a proportion of the population happen to be born with, such as with left-handedness, but that was their aim. Make it so children couldn't be educated about being gay, in an attempt to make sure no child comes out as gay. It is this fundamental ethos of Section 28 that modern British transphobes, and our government, are looking to bring back - but this time for trans children.

This was recently demonstrated during the first 2022 Conservative Party leadership election, of which both 'finalists' have been PM since, when many candidates made anti-trans positions the forefront of their campaigns. Forget the cost-of-living crisis, global warming, or the summer of fully justified industrial action, candidates to be our next Prime Minister have figured out that the real problem is trans people. This ranged from the dangerously petty, such as when handwritten 'Men' and 'Women' signs were taped over gender-neutral toilet facilities at Kemi Badenoch's campaign launch, to downright dangerous, such as Education Secretary Nadhim Zahawi suggesting that teachers should out trans kids to their parents.

Although neither of these two people will be the Prime Minister when this book comes out (unless of course the Tories have a fifth leadership election since 2016 in the next few months from when I am writing), they will almost certainly be involved in the Government – and their ideas and views on trans people and harking back to Section 28 will be present in the Cabinet and potentially even the Premier themselves.

Another former candidate to be Prime Minister actually provides the best case study of this government's desire to stop children being trans. Suella Braverman, the then Attorney General of England and Wales, now once fired but since rehired Home Secretary, produced an entire speech about how schools, under the current legislation in her eyes, should discriminate against children who come out as trans.

She began her speech, made to the conservative think tank Policy Exchange in August 2022, by saying she believes teachers incorrectly think that it is their duty and obligation to be supportive of trans students. She stated that under her reading of the law it doesn't require them to be, rather it requires the opposite. She doubled down on this position by saying that any teacher that supports trans children could be seen as socially transitioning them, a not-so-veiled way of saying that supportive teachers are grooming children to be trans.

After telling teachers not to safeguard their pupils, she listed a series of examples how, under her reading of current law, it is perfectly legal, and indeed right, to discriminate against trans pupils. One example she gave was how it would be right for a girls' school to refuse entry to a trans girl or that mixed schools should not allow a trans girl to use the girls' facilities, as well as how it "can be lawful for a school to refuse to use the preferred opposite-sex pronouns of a trans child".

Equally Braverman views it as the school's duty, just like fellow Conservative Nadhim Zahawi, to inform parents if a child comes out as trans at the school. All this was said by the Attorney General of England and Wales, and as stated, it clearly shows this government's desire to stop children being trans – just as Thatcher's government wanted to stop children being gay. They are looking at what Section 28 was designed to do and copying that ideology with a slight twist, to make it trans-focused. However, they of course won't stop at just attacking trans people, many Tory cabinet members have a history of voting against gay marriage – and they surely will have revoking that in their sights.

One further point of interest on this is that Suella Braverman, despite later attending a fee-paying school, was at a local authority state-funded Primary School during the Section 28 years. Perhaps if she had been taught about the LGBTQIA+ community during those formative years, she would not have so easily fallen for trans-phobic talking points later in her life.

It is undeniable that part of Section 28's legacy is the way the current government wants to take elements from it and re-implement them today. Right now, this is primarily with a focus on the trans community – but there is no reason it won't be extended to all parts of the LGBTQIA+ community.

Thatcher saw restricting what could be taught at schools and making it hard for gay children to be themselves at those schools as a way of eliminating gay people. This government has taken that inspiration, that legacy, and are now trying to use schools as a way of eliminating trans people. It will of course not, quote unquote, "work". There will always be trans children – though it is also undeniable that any moves to bring back these elements of Section 28 will result in a rise in suicides amongst our community.

* * *

Section 28, even though it came off the statute books during my primary school education, had a huge effect on me personally in my journey to understanding and accepting myself – as it did for countless others of my generation and older. This much is obvious. What I would argue is less immediately obvious is the fact that Section 28 has contributed to this current wave of anti-trans hysteria in the present, and that its underlying mechanics are being used as inspiration to target trans children today.

It is a legacy I argue we need to get to terms with so we can best mobilize as a community against the attacks we face today, and future attacks that our future Governments might seek to bring in. However, just as we beat Section 28, we can and will beat any legislation against our community that is brought in by those seeking to attack us. Progress marches forward, and as ever, we won't be left behind.

CHAPTER 2

Out of the Shadows of Section Twenty-Hate

BY CHRIS-JAE ANGEL
(THEY/THEM)

Chris-Jae Angel is a vocal, brown trans non-binary writer, sex worker, activist, podcaster and fashion disaster from Essex, with ethnic roots stemming from South Asia, the Caribbean, Spain…and England.

Content Warnings
Racism, Homophobia, Transphobia

I started senior school in 1998 and the shift from going from an obviously queer kid who was allowed to display their talents in junior school, to one that was lambasted for doing the same here, was something of a shock to the system to me. And as time went on, as they funnelled my life out of me, I was just an empty shell, sitting in classes, because I wasn't allowed to exist as me. I had no-one to reach out to, no understanding of people like me, in so many ways.

I have always known I was queer, from the moment I was born, but being born in '87, the only time I'd see queer people being mentioned in the press, on TV, was accusations of perversion or the heartbreak of the AIDS epidemic. The "we don't want you here" narrative was one I was already aware of from being a BIPOC person. Somehow being authentically myself threatened these people even more, especially in Essex, where I grew up.

As the school years progressed, I became more of an empty shell. I sat through "health" classes being lumped in with cisgender boys to be told by teachers, brazenly, that "pussy is life" and then demanded to raise our hands "if we are fags, because at least two of you in here will be". At this point, even I knew reporting this to heads of the school would achieve nothing, having done so previously and being told I "had imagined" what a teacher had said, despite having another witness with me. It wasn't just stifling, it was crushing and dehumanising.

I somehow scraped through five years of school and left in 2003, after countless incidents with students, and teachers, including being sexually harassed by other kids in my year. And finishing at this time, I could breathe again. But Section 28 caused waves of trauma in many for decades still to come. It's instilled in me to still hold myself back, to still fear. And it's still in many who believed being queer was wrong back then, to still believe it is wrong. We also cannot underestimate how many trans folx, myself included, lost decades of our lives for fear of accessibility to anything about who we are. It cast so many into the shadows and a simple repealing - to give rights that always should have been there - isn't enough when we consider how many we lost through lack of support, understanding and freedom to exist, in the fifteen years it ravaged our communities.

I came out as trans in 2021, after a whole lifetime of knowing exactly who I am. Now is my time to thrive and be beautiful in a world that held us back from being so for long enough. At thirty-five years old, I'm finally able to start living my life and be visible representation for others like me and others that think they could be like me. They don't deserve to be stifled, just like we didn't deserve to be.

CHAPTER 3

Context/Choices

BY ALEX HILTON
(THEY/THEM)

Alex is an autistic author living the West Midlands. In their spare time they enjoy reading and gardening.

Content Warnings
Dysphoria, Religion, Transphobia

I grew up between a homophobic church,
And a school under Section 28,
Cloaked in invisibility,
Not thinking I was OK.

I was in my 20s before I saw,
Anything good about being gay,
I came out, I came out,
I came out so many times,
My attractions told me,
I must be gay.

But bi, queer, trans (nonbinary),
I didn't yet know how to say,
Stuck between the systemic,
And the accidents of place and time,
It's funny how the past sticks with you,
And the pattern recognition it gives you.

Like a flashback-
It doesn't repeat but it rhymes,
The past bleeds into the present, many times,
I didn't choose the context I chose to make my choices in,
So I'm proud of who I became,
although it's not who I would have been.

To the version of me who grew up with visibility:
did you come out early?

Do you still feel like you're catching up
perpetually?

Did you find the love of your life
and start a family?

And what's it like to navigate dysphoria
without patriarchy?

And to celebrate all of us
without inequality?

Does it open up new relational possibilities?

And who did you manage to be,
With enough support for disability?
I've seen the impossible change in my lifetime,
So I know it can change again in mine,
And pain is not the only pattern I recognise.

So I want a body that fits, but in a world that's fair,
And if not, let me be part of the work to get there,
Because stuck between the systemic,
And the accidents of time and space,
We're creating a better context,
To choose to make our choices in.

CHAPTER 4

Lacking a Language

BY ASH BROCKWELL
(HE/THEY)

Ash Brockwell is a non-binary transmasc poet, songworker, artist, educator, parent, and wilderness wanderer. He is the editor of the TransVerse anthology series and author of *Emotional Literacy*.

Content Warnings
Bullying, Mental Health, Dysphoria, Suicidal Thoughts

Recently, while preparing to teach a module on the global climate crisis, I resolved to include some of the voices that are usually unheard. I knew that Indigenous and local knowledge about the natural world, often encoded in the form of songs or stories, was being ignored because it didn't fit the colonial definition of 'knowledge'. I started searching YouTube, looking for videos by community leaders in Africa, Asia, or Latin America that might communicate some of this overlooked expertise and explain where western environmentalists are going wrong.

Yes, I know this is a weird way to start an essay on a 1980s law about sexual orientation. No, I didn't send the wrong document: there's a connection, I promise.

During my search, I found a video on something called 'epistemic oppression' - the 'epistemic' part comes from episteme, the Greek word for knowledge. I discovered that there are three types of epistemic oppression. First-order is when you can communicate your knowledge, but it's not taken seriously because of prejudice against you. Second-order is when you can't communicate what you know to someone else, either because it's so different from their life experience that they can't understand it, or because there isn't a word for it in their language. Third-order epistemic oppression is when you can't even think coherently about what you know, let alone talk about it. That might be because the words don't even exist in your own language, or because you haven't encountered them yet.

The video cited the Black American writer Ta-Nehisi Coates. In his autobiography *Between the World and Me*, Coates talks about growing up in a context of racial inequity without having the language to think or speak about it. He explains that he always knew 'something wasn't right', but didn't have the educational resources yet to explain what it was that was wrong. That quote summed up the first four decades of my life. Without trying to compare Coates' experience of Blackness in a violent white supremacist society to my own privileged upbringing in rural England, I could certainly relate to lacking a language to explain what it was that didn't feel right. It was all thanks to Section 28 and, more broadly, the national conversation around sexuality and gender in the eighties and early nineties.

TRANS, MUTED

We couldn't find ourselves. We searched in vain
on library shelves, in textbooks, TV, movies. Not a trace,
in any place we looked, of any kind of mind
or face or soul that looked like ours. We weren't quite sure,
to tell the truth, what we were looking *for*; we only knew
that something didn't fit. We knew that we were weird,
messed up, abnormal; but we didn't have a word for it.
We feared we'd never learn to get it right
(whatever 'it' was), never quite fit in. We couldn't win.
We tried all options: fight, flight, freeze, or just pretend.
It made no difference, in the end. They'd tease us anyway.

Pretend to smile. Pretend to be OK.
Pretend to be a girl who fancies boys.
Scrawl hearts on all your notebooks. Buy the bras.
Blot lipstick kisses on your posters of the stars
of stage and screen and song. Just fake it
till you make it. Wake up, make-up, play the role.
Keep smiling, that's the goal. Chin up. Stay strong.

Put on the heels. Pretend that nothing's wrong.

Ironic, really, how much we pretended, if the aim
was to protect us from the evil of pretence.
'Pretended family relationships', they claim.
It never *did* make sense.

* * *

I was a transmasculine child in a society that didn't even acknowledge the possibility of transmasculine or non-binary children.
The only options available were 'girl', 'boy' and 'tomboy', and none
of those fitted me properly. 'Tomboy' was the closest, but everyone
knew that tomboys were sporty - and thanks to my undiagnosed
dyspraxia and lack of 3D vision, I was the exact opposite of sporty.
Climbing trees was a non-starter, and attempting to ride a bike was
a disaster. My dad tried to teach me a few times and then declared
that I was useless, which only confirmed to me what I already
thought I knew.

People were always asking me, 'What's the matter?' when I cried,
as I frequently did, but I could never come up with a sensible answer.
Everything was the matter. I was the matter. I was small and nerdy,
with thick unfashionable glasses and sticking-out teeth: I didn't
want to hang out with the girls, and the boys didn't want to hang
out with me. I cried when I dropped the baton at majorettes, went
the wrong way in country dancing, came last in every race, missed
every catch, got picked last for every team, and was the only child
in my ballet class to fail the Grade 2 exam (after scraping through
Grade 1). I cried if I made mistakes on a test at school, even if I still
had the top mark in the class, because it just added yet another layer
of 'wrong' to the overall wrongness of me.

The tears didn't go unnoticed. My primary school bullies, James B, James C, and James D (yes, those were their actual names) nicknamed me 'Living Flood' and sang a parody version of Cliff Richard's *Living Doll* at me: 'Got myself a crying, crying, crying, crying, living flood!' But the song that haunted me the most was a one-liner, repeated over and over by the Jameses: 'Radio 1's a load of crap like [my full deadname, including the middle name].' From that point on, I could never hear my full name without a small voice in my head chanting 'load of crap'.

I'd never been a huge fan of my name in the first place. My mum loved it, and had chosen it even before she was pregnant – convinced she would have a girl, because she never wanted a boy – but it just didn't feel like me. At the age of five, I'd tried my hardest to persuade my family to call me something else. My preferred name was Steven, but everyone laughed at that and told me it was a boy's name, so I kept trying out different alternatives in the hope that something might stick. Whatever the name of the day was, I refused to answer to anything else, until my mum and my favourite aunt took to asking me, 'Who are you today?' instead of asking how I was. At some point my dad told me not to be so stupid, and the name-changing came to an end, but I was still annoyed with my cousin because he was allowed to be Steven and I wasn't.

As a teenager, I quickly gave up on the idea of trying to fit in with the popular girls – shopping for clothes, trying out make-up, and swooning over pop stars didn't interest me at all. Yet I still tried hard to convince myself that I 'fancied' boys, because everyone else seemed to. I had what I thought of as crushes on a few of the boys at school and in my orchestra, but if they'd liked me back and wanted to do anything sexual, I'd have run several miles! Meanwhile,

I was happy to exchange pen-pal letters with a girl who taught me how to say things like 'I kiss you' and 'I love you with all my heart' in Romanian, without it ever occurring to me that this was at all unusual.

By the time I was fourteen, I'd found my place in a quartet of misfits. We were all queer and neurodivergent in one way or another, although we couldn't have identified ourselves that way in the early 1990s: 'queer' was still a slur, and the language of neurodiversity didn't exist yet either. While we never spoke about our queerness, and of course LGBTQIA+ issues were never even mentioned in our school's 'PSE' (Personal and Social Education) classes, we still recognised each other as kindred spirits. One member of the quartet caused a scandal by coming out as gay at sixteen, immediately after leaving school. I was neither brave enough nor self-aware enough: it was another four years before I wrote in my diary, 'I think I might be bisexual' – in code, to make sure my mum didn't read it – and seven years before I dared speak the words aloud.

I'm not convinced I was ever truly bisexual. As with 'tomboy', it was the least-wrong word in the tiny set of available labels. I was always attracted to women and feminine-presenting people, but with varying degrees of denial about my lack of interest in straight cis men. Even the man that I ended up marrying, at the age of 25, was often mistaken for a woman because of his long hair, jewellery, and colourful clothes!

As a result of the repressive environment created by Section 28 during my formative years, it's only now that I'm beginning to make sense of the surreal marriage that took up my late twenties and early thirties. Looking back, I have so many unanswered questions. Did it 'work' for seven years because I was putting in so much effort to learn my husband's language and fit into his culture – while also being heavily brainwashed by a homophobic religious community - that I lost track of who I really was? Did the fact that I was a white foreigner make people more accepting of my gender non-conformity, or more willing to forgive my inevitable 'failure' at womanhood? Did I get away with it for so long because queerness was (and still is) a huge taboo in the country where I was living, to the extent that nobody ever talked about it?

There were days when I thought I was happy, days when I was so unhappy that I wished the overcrowded and badly-driven buses would crash and put me out of my misery, and a lot of days – probably the majority - when I was too busy and too exhausted to feel anything at all. I fled from my own wordless wrongness by cramming my days as full as I could: running my own business, doing charity work, reciting the daily 'obligatory' prayer testifying to my own powerlessness and poverty (in contrast to the power and wealth of God), and brainwashing others to do the same.

Something had to give, and in 2010, everything fell apart. The global economy crashed, the business tanked, the charity was beset by allegations of fraud, my husband's mistress gave birth to his child, and the pretence of happiness became too exhausting to sustain. I accepted a part-time research job at the University of Brighton and came back to the UK as a 32-year-old single parent, almost broken, with two traumatised young children.

It wasn't enough that I'd failed at life, according to almost every definition of failure that I could think of. Without even realising it, I'd positioned myself in the LGBTQIA+ capital of southern England. In a city full of rainbow flags, denying my queerness was no longer an option. Given that I was still a member of the same homophobic cult, though, it was difficult to know what to do with it. Plagued by suicidal thoughts and unrequited love, I wrote this poem and published it under a pseudonym on an anonymous forum:

A LESBIAN'S LOVE/HATE SONG TO GOD

It's thanks to you that I'm alive.
I hate you more with every day.
You almost make me want to die.
I love you more than words can say.

I want to smash your godly face,
but all I do is punch the air.
I want to feel your soft embrace,
but when I sleep there's no-one there.

I want to burn the Holy Book
and throw the ashes in the sea,
But even if I burned the world,
I'd breathe the smoke and there you'd be.

You pin me up against a wall.
There's no way out. There's no way through.
I want to, but I can't. I won't.
I'm leaving her. I'm leaving you.

I can't forget. I can't remember.
Have to. Can't. I won't give in.
I need to. Can't, though. There's no path.
It never works. I just can't win.

So why the hell did you create
a creature wired up all wrong?
I love her. Hate her. Love you. Hate you.
Love that girl and hate this song.

You made my heart. You made the rules.
So what the fuck? Why don't they match?
You tell me love is good. I love her.
What's so bad, then? Where's the catch?

You tell me, "Pray." I've prayed and prayed
until I thought my soul would crack.
Why don't you listen? Can't you hear?
There's no way forward, no way back.

I wish I'd never heard her name.
I wish I'd never heard your voice,
Then I could love her all my life.
I wish I didn't have this choice.

It's thanks to you I want to die.
I hate you more than words can say.
You almost make me feel alive.
I love you more with every day.

* * *

Things started to change when I picked up a business card for a
'spiritual counsellor' in a Brighton café. Following a short course of
therapy and a lot more poems, I started coming out to a few trusted

friends as a lesbian. Something about the word still didn't feel quite right, but it was closer to the truth than 'bisexual' and a thousand times better than pretending to be a straight cis woman. At least I was finally being honest about my attraction to women. One small step at a time, I started to own my queerness: borrowing books from the extensive LGBTQIA+ section in the Jubilee Library, buying *Diva* magazine (when it wasn't on a shelf that was too high for me to reach), and binge-watching *Lip Service* while my parents and children were asleep.

I remember chatting to an openly gay colleague about Section 28 and finding out that it had been repealed while I was living abroad – and later, celebrating with him via text message when same-sex marriage was legalised in England and Wales. With his encouragement I even got brave enough to go to a lesbian meetup event after work, although I was disappointed to discover that the only other attendees were two trans women whose special interest was trainspotting! I love vintage trains just as much as any other former '80s transmasc kid who was told that *Thomas the Tank Engine* was for boys, but writing down the numbers was a step too far for me, and on this occasion I was out-nerded and made an early exit.

As the years went by, and I recovered from the reverse culture shock and embraced the Brighton queer scene, life started to improve. With the help of my spiritual counsellor and the wonderful book *The Artist's Way* by Julia Cameron, I rediscovered my love of painting and found a passion for going on pilgrimages to sacred places. My daughters and I moved out of my parents' basement and into a flat in the New Forest. I even met the love of my life, or so I thought at the time, although sadly she didn't love me in the same way.

The work situation came to a head in the autumn of 2016, when one colleague remarked on feeling uncomfortable with her granddaughter's nursery displaying pictures of same-sex couples, and another told me I should pray more and see a doctor about my sexual orientation. They both belonged to the same religious group as I did, and clearly expected me to agree with the party line. This coincided with a change to the train schedule that made my commute from the New Forest to Brighton even more unmanageable. Fuck this, I thought. I handed in my notice and started a freelance consulting company, with only one client on my books and not even the faintest hint of a business plan. On the day I left the office for the last time, I came out as a lesbian to all my friends and family. It was still the best approximation that I had. Thanks to the train-spotters, I knew about transgender women, but I'd never knowingly encountered a trans man or a non-binary person.

Quitting my job without a proper back-up plan was one of the bravest, stupidest, and best decisions I ever made. With a buyer showing serious interest in the house that I owned with my ex-husband, I turned my attention to writing songs and a full-length novel, instead of looking for new clients. My ex later pulled out of the deal, rented the house out, and kept all the rental income – but by the time I realised how dire my financial situation had become, and started wishing that I had taken the business more seriously, the first draft was already complete.

The novel was a game-changer, not because I sold it to a publisher and solved all my money problems – to this day, I still haven't published it – but because it gave me a safe way to explore the concept of gender transition before confronting the issue of my own gender. What began as a lesbian historical romance soon acquired a life of its own, with a minor character (who happened to be transmasculine) falling in love with the heroine and then increasingly taking over the plot! In the first draft, my poor hero was subjected to all manner of humiliation and abuse that reflected my internalised transphobia. As the year went on, though, my research started feeling more and more personal. In parallel, my character gradually became more nuanced and convincing with each round of editing, and his story arc less traumatic.

Without telling anyone, I started joining Facebook groups for non-binary people. My vocabulary grew quickly, and so did my self-awareness. A few weeks after my fortieth birthday, I woke up with my new full name. It was a strange experience, in that there was no process of 'choosing' a name, and I don't have any conscious recollection of dreaming it. I woke up one day, looked in the mirror, and said to myself, 'I'm Ashley Jay Brockwell' – immediately followed by a sense of recognition: 'Oh, *that's* who I am!'

On reflection, my name made a lot of sense in the context of my spiritual practice, which had become more and more nature-based since my dramatic flounce from the homophobic cult. *Ash*, in the Druid tradition, is one of the three most sacred trees. The Oak is associated with the Sacred Masculine, and the Hawthorn with the Sacred Feminine, but ash? Well, I couldn't find a clear reference to gender, but the fact that they were always a triad – with Ash in the middle – clearly implied 'non-binary'. *Ley* is a word used in some pagan and 'new age' traditions to refer to earth energies. *Jay* is a bird that, at least in its British version, resembles a trans flag with wings (the American blue jay is very different). *Brock* is the old English name for the badger, an animal whose black-and-white striped face and grey body felt like the perfect metaphor for a non-binary person. And how does it all end? *Well*. I couldn't have planned it better if I'd tried. Somehow, my subconscious had conjured up a name that brought together the things I'd always loved: trees, the land, birds, animals, water, and healing.

I resolved to change my name on 31 March 2018, which was not only the Spring Equinox full moon – a time symbolising resurrection and rebirth – but also International Transgender Day of Visibility. In practice, I couldn't hold out that long, and started my social transition on New Year's Eve instead. I opened a new Facebook page under the name Ashley Jay Brockwell, announced my pronouns as they/them, and shifted the focus of my consultancy business from project evaluation to LGBTQIA+ advocacy and training.

There were still a few plot twists to come. After a few months as a 'they', I started experimenting with 'he/him' pronouns, and realised that felt more comfortable and natural for me. I dropped the middle part of my name in everything other than professional publications and my email address (having already published my PhD as Ashley Jay Brockwell, I didn't want to confuse readers by changing it again!) and became Ash Brockwell, which had a more masculine feel to it. I tried calling myself a man for a while, but that didn't quite fit either.

It was probably around the middle of 2019 that I settled on the words I'm using now to talk about my identity: transmasculine genderflux (or just transmasculine or transmasc flux), queer, demisexual, femmeromantic. The 'flux' part means that I think of my gender identity as fluctuating, but only on a spectrum between male and agender (having no gender) – never female. 'Demisexual' means I don't usually experience sexual attraction unless I've first established an emotional or spiritual bond with the person – although there are exceptions to every rule, and to my great surprise, I met one recently. 'Queer', once a slur, has been reclaimed and is now widely used as a catch-all term for the LGBTQIA+ community – and sometimes, more specifically, for people who resist boxes and labels. Apologies to anyone who still struggles with it, but it works for me. As for 'femmeromantic', I'm not even sure it's a word at all – the official term for attraction to women is 'gyneromantic', which, for me, has dysphoria-inducing associations with gynaecology. But why shouldn't I invent new words if the established ones don't quite fit? For me, 'femmeromantic' does what it says on the tin. I tend to be romantically attracted to feminine-presenting people, including some cis women, some people who were announced female at birth but now identify as non-binary femmes, some transfeminine people, and some trans women.

2019 was also the year when I took my first tentative steps into the world of performance poetry, with an initial gig at the Art House in Southampton as part of their 'Art SO Trans' festival. I read this poem:

YOUR 'AFAB' DOES NOT ERASE ME

Yes, I was assigned-female-at-birth,
grew up behind net curtains with my secrets concealed inside,
where nobody (and least of all me)
understood quite what was denied.
I refused to answer to my given name at five,
hid growing curves under baggy sweaters at twelve,
felt weird and wrong
around girls who wore make-up and heels
and spent their weekends shopping for pink lace bras:
that was all I knew. There were things that I never tried to do,

because it just wasn't 'done', within that net; and many things
that I didn't say, and couldn't have said, however I tried,
because the words weren't even invented yet.
There wasn't a language, then, for people like me.
#TransgenderBoy and #TransgenderMan were years away,
The teachers could have been fired just for saying 'gay'.
So, in conclusion: secrets: kept.

Yet your 'AFAB' cannot define me now.
#WontBeErased #WontBeDenied
My #ExistenceIsResistance;
and if you dare try to delete me, I WILL resist.
Assigning pink lace flowers to hide what you can't accept
can no more erase the blue core of a #TransGuy like me
than King Canute's command 'Thus far, and no further'
could ever hold back the inrushing Solent tide.

Whatever you choose to call me,
whatever you say, I will ride the waves
to places you never dreamed, and live my self-made life
as my truest self anyway.   There's no way in again, now I'm out.
Because this is who I am, and have always been,
and the only alternative is...
No.
 Let's not go there.

I am here.
Defiantly turquoise.
Dynamic.
Impassioned.
Alive.

So take your eraser, take your net curtains, and go;
I am still here, no longer silent, at this meeting-place
of sea and shore, persistently pushing on as the waves do,
and reminding myself day after day that there are more
ways than one to be a man. There are more ways than one
for the deep essence of a human soul to survive.

* * *

It's been a long road from lacking a language to finding my own. It could all have been so much easier and less traumatic if I'd grown up in an era when diverse sexualities and gender identities were normalised and accepted. But despite all the improvements in the past few decades in relation to sexual orientation, there's a very real danger that progress could be reversed when it comes to gender identity. This is largely due to a noisy campaign by a small group of self-styled 'gender-critical feminists' or 'trans-exclusionary radical feminists' – backed up by a motley crew of celebrities and American evangelicals – who insist on framing the rights of trans people and cis women as mutually exclusive. It's as though equality is pie and there's not enough for everyone.

To be more precise, gender-critical folks are insisting that the rights of trans *women* and cis women are mutually exclusive. They rarely talk about trans men or transmasculine people, probably because acknowledging our existence highlights a fatal flaw in their argument. If, as they claim, trans women are men - and therefore belong in men's toilets, changing rooms, prisons, homeless shelters, sports competitions, etc. - the obvious conclusion is that trans men are women and belong in women's spaces. Anyone who has ever met a trans man, especially one who has been on testosterone for several years and has acquired a beard, a moustache, and a deep voice, would be quick to dispute that position. So, too, would nearly all trans men and transmasc people!

I can't speak for everyone, but for me, being forced back into women's spaces after a full social transition would make me feel extremely uncomfortable. That might seem illogical, given that I was raised as a girl and spent most my life in women's spaces – but when a sense of being permanently 'wrong', 'fucked-up' or 'a failure' is finally replaced by a feeling of rightness, there's no going back. Gender dysphoria is hard to explain to anyone who hasn't experienced it, but an analogy might be helpful. If you can imagine spending your entire childhood locked in a tiny room like the young hero of Emma Donohue's novel *Room*, being let out to live your life, and then being sent back to the dreaded room again – that might give you some idea of why the idea of organising public spaces according to 'biological sex' horrifies me so much. (In any case, the binary idea of 'biological sex' as male/penis/XY vs. female/vagina/XX is only meaningful to people with a very limited understanding of biology: the diversity of genes, hormones, bodies, and brains is vastly more complex).

To go back to where I began: epistemic oppression occurs when people can't articulate their lived experiences, aren't understood, or aren't taken seriously because of prejudice against them. This is what Section 28 normalised, and it's happening again, with the emergence of anti-trans propaganda that echoes the 'Gay = AIDS = Death' panic of the 1980s – as well as an increasing backlash against trans rights activists and even cis male drag performers. Trans people have been blamed for everything from the COVID pandemic to the war in Ukraine, even as we continue to insist that we have nothing against cis women, no desire to take any rights away from them, no plan to expose ourselves to them in public places, and no issue with them describing themselves as women. We don't want to start a 'culture war': we just want to be treated with basic human dignity and respect.

If you're a trans / non-binary person reading this, I'm sending you solidarity and strength, with a side helping of apology for anything that you might have found painful or difficult to read.

If you're a cis person, which is statistically much more likely because trans people are a tiny minority of the population, the message I want to leave you with is this: being trans is not a choice, a phase, or a millennial trend. It's an integral part of our identity, and trying to deny it or hide it causes us immense pain. We don't need you to understand fully: we just need you to be there to listen, support us, advocate for us on the days when we're too exhausted or emotionally drained to speak up for ourselves, treat us with dignity, and give us the space to figure things out in our own time.

We might not always have had a language to express who we are; we might still be exploring and experimenting with new words. I can't promise that the words I'm using now to describe my identity are the same words that I'll be using in ten years, five years, or even one year's time. But what I can promise is to show up as authentically as I can, using the words available to me.

Meanwhile, my struggle against epistemic oppression is your struggle too. Humans were never meant to fit into neat binary boxes, and there's always more to a person than words can express. I'm not just a transmasculine demisexual queer femmeromantic person. I'm also a parent, a teacher, an artist, a writer, a poet, a publisher, a

singer, a facilitator, an activist, a wilderness wanderer... etc., etc., etc.
The fact that I happen to be transgender takes nothing away from
any of the above.

So please, whoever and wherever you are, let's stand together.
In celebrating the repeal of Section 28, let's do everything we can
to make sure that 'don't say gay' isn't quietly replaced by 'don't say
trans'. And, on that note...

HERE WE GO AGAIN

(sung to the tune of *Here It Is Again* by The Beautiful South)

Here we go again, just like before,
We're the favoured targets in the culture war;
Here we go again - so don't say 'gay',
Oh, there's more words now you're not allowed to say:
So, let's start with 'trans' and 'non-binary',
Then 'pronouns' – don't YOU agree?
'Protect trans kids' is the devil's phrase,
And 'affirming'? Get in the sea!
You can get in the sea! Don't try to brainwash me!
And if you call me 'cis'... But surely speech is free?

Now we know who we love,
And yet you won't allow us to be just who we are?
Oh yes, we're L-G-B, but don't forget the T,
Why can't we be just who we are?

Here we go again, with a new disguise,
Section 28 through modern eyes:

Here we go again, and I feel so ill:
See the war on blockers, and the bathroom bill!
Heads, *he's autistic and hence not trans,*
Tails, *he must be mad;*
Heads, *she'll detransition,*
Tails, *well, I blame the dad,*
Yes, I blame the dad, no, I blame the mum,
But I've prayed for them all, so don't be glum...

Now we know who we love,
And yet you won't allow us to be just who we are?
Oh yes, we're L-G-B, but don't forget the T,
Why can't we be just who we are?
Just who we are
Just who we are
Just who we are
Just who we are...

CHAPTER 5

An Interview with a Friend

BY BETH WATSON
(ANY)
AND CLAIRE BEVERIDGE
(SHE/HER)

Beth Watson is the founder of Bechdel Theatre CIC, and creator of Queer Diary - where LGBTQIA+ people read their teenage diaries on stage. Beth's debut show, Hasbian, is a comedy about growing up in the UK's 'gay capital' during Section 28.

Claire Beveridge is a marketing consultant for the technology industry. She lives in Vancouver, Canada, with her wife and two cats. Claire can be found cycling, cooking, and hoping Brighton & Hove Albion will one day win the Premier League.

INTRODUCTION

Claire:
My name's Claire. I'm 35, and I live in Vancouver, Canada. I run my own B2B marketing studio that specializes in the software and tech industry.

Beth:
I'm Beth, and I'm also 35. I live in South London and work as a performer, theatre-maker, facilitator, and drag king.

BRIGHTON

Beth:
We both grew up in Brighton, the "gay capital" of the UK. I remember Brighton as a hippy city. It was described in the Angus, Thongs, and Full-Frontal Snogging book, and the author, who was from Brighton, described it as "The San Francisco of the UK".

Claire:
That's so funny! My Canadian wife recently went to Brighton for the first time, and that's exactly what she said: "I feel like I'm in San Francisco!". I was like, "Okaaaay..."

Beth:
San Francisco, but less palm trees!

Claire:

I lived in Patcham for 12 years, which is a suburb of Brighton. Then I moved to Hove (actually...), where I lived until I was 18. I also remember it being... hippy is the right word. And very liberal.

I remember being at one of the first Pride events in Brighton, which was held at The Level (a small patch of grass next to a skate park). I have a memory of going to one of the first-ever Pride events there. Not the first ever. But a very small, young pride.

My Mum is a lesbian, so I was exposed to Brighton's queerness and otherness at a very young age, which I'm incredibly grateful for. So, I always knew Brighton as being synonymous with acceptance, tolerance, politically left-leaning, and welcoming. Then you put that in reflection with Section 28, which goes against all those things...

I pretty much lived in Brighton my entire life until I was 29. Then I moved to Vancouver, which is quite like Brighton—very liberal and very gay.

Beth:
I didn't have a queer parent, but my parents had friends who were gay and lesbian. Then Pride moved to Preston Park. The area of Brighton I'm from is 5 minutes walk from Preston Park, where Pride was held from, I think, the late-90s?

My parents would take me down, and they'd know people involved. I remember my Mom having gay friends who she'd say hi to. It felt like a family, community festival.

Claire:

It's so nice that we both grew up in households where being queer, being gay, being different was so accepted. I felt completely supported by my parents - I dunno whether you felt differently?

Beth:
No. I mean... I was a bit jealous of you having a gay Mom!

My parents were like, "do whatever you want, be whatever you want!". But I think they didn't assume that I was anything other than straight, particularly.

My Mom gave me the biology talk: "Here's the sperm and the egg", and I was like, "Uggh!". Then "Don't ask, don't tell" was the story with ALL sex. I didn't talk about girls. But also didn't talk about boys, didn't tell them I was going out with a boy. It was like... that's your private life. I respected the fact that they taught me to draw lines around my private life without being like, "I'm a cool Mom! Who are you going out with now?"

But it also meant I had limited opportunities to share that side of myself with them. Because I wasn't encouraged to talk about sex and sexuality and it seemed very linked to talking about queerness.

Claire:
That's great - not everyone wants a Mom who's gonna be all up in your shit, y'know? It's nice that they installed those sense of boundaries in you.

Beth:
Was your Mom like that?

Claire:

She never really pried. If I told her anything, it was on my terms more than anything else.

She knew I was 15, 16, out being safe, having fun, living my life. I think honestly, she was just happy that I had friends and I'd met people who were different, like me, who were accepting me for who I was.

SCHOOL

Claire:
Beth and I went to different schools but on the same campus. What was your school like?

Beth:
Dorothy Stringer was a former Secondary Modern at the bottom of a hill. It was a massive, co-ed school. While I was there, it became a Sports College, much to my disgruntlement, because I didn't like sports! That's how it got funding, and now it's an excellent, outstanding school, I've heard. When I was there, it was still in a bit of a transition period from being this Secondary Modern school, a bit under-funded, under-supported. It was on its way to becoming a quite good, sought-after state school. What about you?

Claire:
I went to Varndean at the top of the hill. I started there in 1998. I was massively into sports. Very athletic, played football for Brighton and Hove, in the youth women's team. I played rugby, basketball, hockey, whatever! Varndean was a Technology College. Funny, I work in the technology industry now, but at the time, I couldn't give

two shits about making some graphic design thing on a computer! I just did not care.

I always felt a lot of regret for not going to Dorothy Stringer. From my perspective, Dorothy Stringer was cool as fuck. Stringer was like, where all the Queerdos went. All the arts kids. All the queer people that I ended up meeting, that's where they went.

So I was very jealous of anyone who went to Stringer. To me, it was this sort of utopia at the bottom of the hill. I thought going to Stringer would be a very different experience than being at Varndean.

But actually, our experiences of Section 28 were essentially that we were both under that law. Right?

So how different would it have actually been? Teachers at Varndean were not permitted to talk about homosexuality, and that rule still applied to Stringer. But for me, it was a sense that there was a queer community at Dorothy Stringer, and there wasn't where I was. I found that very, very hard.

Beth:
I don't think there was much of a difference in the schools. I think it was a weird stroke of luck that enabled us to build a little community.

I think there were teachers at Stringer that, as the years went on, I'd recognise as queer. Whether they were deliberately signalling or not, we'd recognise them.

There was one teacher we saw at Pride wearing little gold hot pants! We were like, "Oh my God!". We absolutely knew what he was about. We were in the eco club—so nerdy! He was one of the teachers who ran it. We were like, "We see you! We recognize a nerdy gay." Then there he was, at Pride. And we were like "Yes!!!"

Claire:
That's so validating.

Beth:
So validating! But also weird that they weren't allowed to talk about it.

The teachers would get homophobia, the kids would be like, "You gay, sir?". And they wouldn't be able to say "Yes". So weird.

They didn't create a safe environment because... well, maybe they tried? But weren't able to?

I think your perception of Stringer probably came from luck-of-the-draw that a few of us were in the same form groups or friendship groups. We built a sense of safety. We felt able to form a little band of weirdos.

Claire:
There's definitely something to be said for safety in numbers. When there's a gang of 10 of you who identify as LGBTQIA+?

I knew of one gay guy in my school, Michael, and that was it. There was no one else I felt like I could really relate to, who was different, like me, or had an inkling that they might be attracted to women or, y'know, gay. So that was disappointing.

What were your teachers like, apart from the obvious gay eco-warrior?

Beth:
There were more teachers I assume were gay.

One teacher used to flip out if anyone used "gay" as a derogatory term. He used to YELL—in quite an intense way—if anyone was like, "That's so gay". Which everyone did all the time. Including us!

Claire:
I remember using the word gay or lesbian. It was all "That's so gay!" or "You lesbian!"

Beth:
That's so gay, you're so gay, everything's gay. There was such a trend of using that word.

Once we kind of figured out who we were, I think some of us were like, "WE'RE allowed to say that!" But it's still very ick! Nowadays, I'm like, God, did I really think I could reclaim using gay as a slur? No! Don't do that.

So, we had this teacher who used to flip out about that. And he was a big fan of the pop star Cher. He used to put on Cher if we'd done well in the lesson. As a reward!

He used to say, this sticks with me forever, "don't use gay as a slur because my sister is a lesbian."

Claire:
Hmm.

Beth:
He was American, only at our school for a year on exchange. He'd obviously been told, "You're not allowed to say you're gay in school"

Claire:
Wow.

Beth:
So he's saying, "My sister is a lesbian".

He'd tell us about his "sister". He'd say: "My sister has a pink triangle sticker on her car. Do you know what the pink triangle is?" We'd be like, "Never heard of it."

And he'd be like, "It's a gay flag, a symbol to show other people you're gay. If you see someone waving that flag, it might mean they're gay."

Now I'm like, duh! He was trying to slip some queer education under the radar!

Claire:
A bit of subliminal messaging.

Beth:
Not even subliminal. Just messaging!

But there were some awful teachers. One led an anti-abortion class and gave out those badges with little feet on them, promoting anti-abortion stuff. It wasn't a religious school. It was a bog standard state school. So odd that we had those teachers and some who were probably queer? Or allies... one teacher didn't shave her armpits; she felt like a safe pair of hands!

Claire:
Looking back, I definitely had gay teachers. There was a gay languages teacher, a gay science teacher. And I knew what a gay man was. I was very aware of homosexuality. I just knew. There was a gay art teacher. A lesbian French teacher.

It's weird to think back because I feel like I knew, and they knew. But neither of us could communicate in any way.

There was no safe teacher, conversation, or anyone within the school realm that I could turn to when I was having a hard time. So that created quite an unsafe environment.

Once, by chance, when I was 20 or 21 after I'd left school, I was in a club in Brighton, and I randomly bumped into an old art teacher who was out clubbing. I went up to him and said, "Oh my gosh, it's Mr. So-and-so! Do you remember me?" He was like, "Of course I remember you". He got really emotional and kind of... he didn't hold me, but he was sort of sad?

He saw how I was treated, and I did not have a great time at school at all in terms of homophobic bullying. He said, "It was the hardest thing, watching people be so horrible to you, and I couldn't do anything about it." And he cried. You could see his inner turmoil.

I had a hard time at school. But seeing it from a teacher's perspective, now, as a 35-year-old adult. My wife's a teacher, y'know? You think, holy shit. That must have been so difficult for them as well. To see his internal heartbreak, that he couldn't do more for me, couldn't have supported me? That was so moving and really, really sad to see his upset at not being able to help, not just me but the one other gay guy in my school year as well.

I think it helps sum up the impact of Section 28. It wasn't just students, it was teachers as well. All so impacted by this God-awful law.

I came out when I was 14, in Year 9, I remember just saying, "I'm a lesbian, and I've got a girlfriend". I think because I always looked different... I was a complete tomboy, only wore boys' clothes, and I was sporty, so I think I was a prime target, whether I came out or not, as being different. That was it.

I got married this summer, and my Mom, at the party, was regaling my friends with some of my stories from school. And I learned something.

When I was 15, I tore some ligaments in my knee. I was a massive soccer player, so I was distraught. It was the end of my football career. I had my whole leg in plaster, and I was on crutches. So, apparently, and I don't remember this, but someone in a corridor pushed me over and said, "You fucking crippled tranny." And my response was...I got up, and I beat this kid with a crutch. I was like, "Don't talk to me like that. Fuck off". I got in so much trouble for violent behaviour. Nothing happened to him for homophobia. Absolutely nothing. It was like it didn't happen.

I was in classes where I was removed. I had to sit on my own in an office because the bullying that went on was too much for teachers to handle. They were like, "The only way that we can solve this problem is if we segregate Claire", essentially.

I had no idea about the segregation until my mom told me 4 or 5 weeks ago, not at the wedding; she didn't bring up the trauma! But my friends were saying, "Your Mom was saying how brave you were. You always stood up for yourself and didn't give a shit whether you were in trouble or not cause you knew what was happening was wrong". And I was like, "Oh, I didn't look at it like that." I look at it like, "Oh my God, I had this awful time". But maybe I was showing a lot of character, a lot of strength?

My Mom said, "You had no idea how often I was in the school, talking to teachers, saying, what's going on is homophobic bullying. Something needs to be done". But the pushback was, "Our hands are tied. We can't do anything about this. We just have to get through it.". And I think that's what happened.

I don't really see myself going to high school. I feel like I survived high school.

Beth:
It's amazing to have a Mum who will fight that fight.

I wonder if you had the words to say, "I'm going out with a girl, I'm a lesbian," because you had that representation within your family? Like, not in pop culture or... well, not in school, because like we weren't allowed.

Claire:
I think it must've been. Probably subconsciously, because at the time, me and my Mum did not get on. Cause obviously, I was a 14-year-old, moody teenager!

But I think maybe I knew that there was someone advocating for me. And I knew that actually, being a lesbian, there's nothing wrong with it. Because I grew up in a lesbian household. So I was exposed to it, maybe? And subconsciously, I knew that there was always someone fighting. So yeah, potentially.

Did you experience homophobia in your school?

Beth:
I was really badly bullied in Primary School, including in ways I now identify as homophobic. At the time, I was "A Weirdo", but you called our friendship group "The Queerdos", and I think that goes hand-in-hand with the fact that my being bullied - for being "different" - was loaded in a particular way.

When I was in Primary School, as young as 8 or 9, I had girls in the changing room like, "Eugh, don't look at me! Are you a paedo? Are you gay? Do you fancy me?". I wasn't a tomboy; I hated sports! I think I just gave off a vibe that I wasn't the same.

Claire:
Mmm-hmm

Beth:
For me, it's hard to identify what was homophobic. Because, retrospectively, I was also neurodivergent. I was undiagnosed with various social and learning-related things that weren't known to teachers—they didn't have time to diagnose us. I could read, so they wouldn't worry. That was the level of support - "You can read! You're fine!"

But I experienced a similar thing to you, in Primary, my Mom would come in and say to teachers, "My kid's being bullied". She didn't say homophobic. But bullies would ask: "Did you used to be a man? Why are your arms so hairy? Show us your willy!". Now I realize that's probably an early sense that something was different about me.

Claire:
Mmm-hmm.

Beth:
My Mom said, "Beth's being targeted repeatedly, left out of everything. What the hell are you gonna do?" But the teachers said, "That's in the playground, not for us to deal with. It's not our business. Kids call each other names!"

I also used to lash out when I was being bullied. I would smack them, then get in loads of trouble for being out of control, and having a bad temper. I just... I knew that it was wrong, I had this intense pressure building up. I had to be quiet, shut up, and stay by myself in the playground. Avoid the changing room. Avoid PE. Sit in my corner. I had a terrible time at Primary School. My parents let me not go in much for the final year cause I had such a horrible time and no friends.

I think that's why, when I came to Secondary School, I was like... tough as nails. I got one of those bomber jackets with the orange inside when I got to Year 7. I wore it like armour.

And I would punch people. But I was very, very small. The bullies were twice the size of me, with my little bomber jacket!

I think because I was directly told, teachers cannot defend you, teachers are refusing to protect you. So when I got to Secondary School, I cast myself as like - the defender of the weirdos.

That was part of the reason I ended up with this crowd of friends. I was like, "Don't mess. I'll deck you if you say anything to my friend. If you shout Dyke at my friend, I will come at you!". I think because it happened to me earlier.

I have always been aware, though, that I am scarred, on a very deep level. Because of how early it happened. As an adult, I have self-doubt, a distrust of people, that originates from Primary School trauma. And, y'know, gender and sexuality stuff that comes from this really deeply-lodged bullying.

But because it happened early, I was ready for homophobic bullying. I handled school.

When a kid in Secondary School said, "Are you a man?" I'd be like, "So what if I am? Deal with it". As soon as I started getting "You fucking dyke, you lesbian. Are you a goth? Do you eat babies?" I'd go, "Yes. All of the above. With relish."

Claire:
It's so empowering. For someone in Year 7, that's such a nice story.

SECTION 28

Beth:
I don't remember finding out Section 28 existed. I don't remember a penny-dropping moment! Whenever I found out, I think it

made so much sense, it was as if I'd always known. There was an official level of taboo around LGBTQIA+ stuff in school, so it made sense that there was a law.

Also, the amount of Tory-hating in the house I grew up in, generally among people that I spent time around - meant the origin of the law was no surprise. I knew that Margaret Thatcher was a Big Bad.

Do you remember finding out Section 28 was a thing?

Claire:
I definitely learned about it later in life. There wasn't any pinnacle moment that I remember, like a "Holy shit!". But in agreement with you, looking back, it totally makes sense.

Especially the way homophobia was dealt with within my school in particular. You can now look back, and I can see why I was labelled the problem, versus the homophobic bullying being the problem.

At the time, I didn't have any understanding of why I was being segregated from a classroom to stop homophobic bullying when they should have been tackling the issue. So it was interesting to learn that that rule was in place. It puts so much into context, making you re-contextualise your high school experience.

In this day and age, being queer is hot shit. You're like, fucking cool if you are queer. It's so accepted. Everyone's got a gay best friend. It's the norm. So yeah. I definitely was not aware of Section 28 at the time. But later in life, it came into more prominence and helped frame a few experiences.

Beth:

I remember, in recent years, finding out details. Such as, Section 28 sounded like something ancient! Something from the olden days, right? But it's only in the last 5 years that I found out it was introduced in 1988. The year after I was born.

Claire:
Oh, holy shit.

Beth:
Then it went on until 2003! I had an awareness at school that the age of consent was different for men who have sex with men, to women and men having sex. I also knew that there was no law against lesbian sex because Queen Victoria didn't believe it existed. At every opportunity, I'd be like, "It's not illegal, ha!". So I knew those laws.

But I assumed Section 28 was older than the 80s. Like, from the 60s when homosexuality was criminalised? Or the 70s? Pre-my lifetime! But it was 1988.

Now I know about AIDS, and the way that was handled by the Tory government. I know that's where it originated. But the way it mapped onto my birth. Then didn't go away until...

Claire
2003! The year we graduated high school. Our whole childhood and teenage experiences governed by this law.

Beth:
And considering the Labour government was such a big thing when we were kids, y'know? Tony Blair coming in was gonna fix it

all! Make everything better! The fact that it still existed for so long was and still is wild.

Claire:
Labour got voted in, in '97, right? Then governed for how long?

Beth:
Until 2010.

Claire:
That in itself is surprising. We think of 1980, it still feels like it wasn't that long ago. I was born in '86. You were born in...

Beth:
'87.

Claire:
You think, gosh. How can that be? But then you see what's happening in the States at the moment. You see these laws that we think are gonna protect us, be there for us forever... you see how quickly these things can be taken away.

I'd be very, very concerned that something like Section 28 could eventually come around again. I don't think it will. But looking at what's happening in America: Roe versus Wade, there's the threat against marriage equality. Everything that's happening. Things can go backward quite fast.

Beth:
I think there's a false sense of security in seeing politics as this continual progression towards socially liberal values. I think that's a

distraction from the fact that anything could change at any minute. Particularly in this country, in the UK, everything happening around trans rights is terrifying.

Liz Truss just became Prime Minister, and she's very transphobic. She's a wannabe Thatcher. Dresses up as her. She's keen to weaponize what she calls "culture wars" and uses similar rhetoric to Margaret Thatcher around "protecting children" as an excuse for curtailing rights for trans people. I wouldn't be surprised if she, or someone like her, were to bring in some kind of law about trans... everything, trans rights, trans healthcare, trans people existing in schools. It feels very Thatcherite.

I'm seeing huge echoes, looking at Section 28 because I've been making a show set in this era I've been looking at speeches, seeing through lines in ways politicians talk about trans people as a "threat to society". It's really scary.

Claire:
I'm so shocked by that. Maybe it's living here in Vancouver. Being very honest, I read *The Guardian* every now and then, but I don't really follow much UK news anymore cause I've lived in Canada for 7 years. The treatment of trans people, especially here on the West Coast, is so accepting. I could not imagine something like that happening in Canada. Especially in Vancouver. So to hear that is so alarming and shocking.

I really, really hope that we don't go back to a law like Section 28 that will impact trans people. But that's such a valid point to raise.
How do you think your experiences under 28 impacted you as an adult?

Beth:

I think I have self-doubt. But also a thick skin that you get from having to defend yourself and a strong sense of the value of community. Because of having to find our own education, our own pop culture. It gave me a sense of embracing difference. The independence of having to seek out our own stuff. The idea that no one's gonna take us to see *But I'm A Cheerleader*—we had to go ourselves!

Claire:

That's great. What an amazing film, as well. I think for me my experiences of bullying left me with a lot of anger, distrust, and some social anxiety. A lot of alcohol and drug misuse—especially at 16, 17... I was off the rails. I think I always found a lot of solace in drinking a lot of alcohol, and I gave that up about 2 years ago. I think I used it predominantly as a crutch, to help me feel more accepted around other people. And I'm a very confident person. I have a lot of faith in myself, I hold myself in very high regard! But I also have had periods of incredibly low self-esteem.

I think those experiences of High School really pushed me down a path that I shouldn't have gone down. It reframed the world I live in and shaped me in a way that wasn't meant to happen. But I'm really, really proud of myself for being able to build a nice successful life and get over those challenges.

Beth:

I feel like I've spent my entire adulthood avoiding drugs. I saw people get into them in Sixth Form, and I knew that if I went anywhere near that direction, I'd be absolutely absorbed. I definitely have a... not dependent, but a relationship with drinking. It's a part of my life I turn to for confidence. I think that's something that we have in common; thinking of what we were like as teenagers, we were building this front of being a real tough guy.

Claire:
Totally.

Beth:
Being a bit of a badass, a bit of a player.

Claire:
Yeah. Not a rebel, but I think you and I were similar, we were very extroverted and exuded a lot of confidence, but it took a lot for people to see underneath the facade. And we still have incredibly big problems with being vulnerable. I don't really like exposing my inner true self because I'm scared. I'm scared that people are gonna turn around and hurt me.

I think, potentially, we were of a similar ilk growing up. There was a lot of bravado, and a lot of confidence, for sure. But inside, we were both struggling quite massively.

Beth:
Yeah. When I tell people about my teenage self, people are like, "Wow, I wish I was like you as a teenager; you were so confident, so outspoken, so sure of yourself". But I see how vulnerable I was, how doubtful. Even though I never doubted my sexuality—well, never thought I was a heterosexual! But it didn't mean that I was always okay with it. It just meant: "Oh God, I just have to deal with this. I can't show any weaknesses. They'll attack me. The whole world is against me because everyone hates us."

Claire:
I think you do build up a thicker skin. Did you ever go to Allsorts?

Beth:
No! I was like, "Why do you need a youth club to be gay? Can't you just be gay out in the world? Why do you need to, like, go to a club? Sounds gay to me!". Thought I didn't need a group because I was soooo well adjusted!

Claire:
I told my Mom, "I'm going to this youth club." She was like, "Oh right. What one is that then?" And I said, "Allsorts". Of course, she knew what Allsorts was. She was like, "I think that's really good for you."

She recently said, "Do you remember how you used to meet up?". She said, "The first time you went to Allsorts, you had to meet them somewhere totally random. Two of the leaders wanted to meet you in person, like outside the Pier or something. They didn't give out the address in case homophobes came to cause damage, mischief". They had to tell kids, "You can meet us at 2 o'clock, at the Pier. Then we'll take you to the location."

Beth:
Wow. I never knew that.

Claire:
The level of safety. Now you think that's bizarre! This was not pre-internet.. but you couldn't just look up anything. Now,

nothing's hidden. But there was this level of safety and security around this LGBTQIA+ youth group. Which was very well played by them. But also shows you where things were, actually.

Beth:
How did you find out about Allsorts?

Claire:
So, I noticed Laura walking home from school one day. Everyone from Stringer used to walk up the hill past Varndean, and I'd seen her with Christina. I thought she was the most beautiful person I'd ever seen, basically.

Beth:
I mean, she was.

Claire:
She was absolutely stunning. I could tell she was different... like, a lesbian. We didn't use the word queer then, y'know? It was "I'm a lesbian". Queer wasn't in our lexicon! I was like, "I have to get to know her." That's how we started dating. And she was like, "You should come to this!" That's how that all began. That was my gateway into going to Allsorts and learning that there were other people like yourself, Laura, and Christina, who identified as bi, gay, lesbian, queer, whatever. So that's how I then became friends with you and everyone else.

Beth:
It's weird how Section 28 looms as this huge national travesty. When so much of its impact was so small, so insidious. I feel like the impact of it was harder for the fact that we didn't know about it.

For all our fighting at school, we didn't quite know about the bigger picture that we were fighting.

We were ready to punch any bully that came in our path. But we didn't understand that there was like, a big, bad bully in the form of legislation that was actually doing the most intense damage. It still echoes in our lives today, I think.

I don't feel like, as an adult, I've ever had a moment of "I've come out now! That plaster has been ripped off. I can get on with my life!" It's a constant process (coming out) because of the level of assumptions people make about each other, about sex, sexuality, and gender. The lack of understanding.

Even at that age, we were versed in like, being gay, stuff like that. But we didn't have the knowledge to see ourselves as a bigger part of kind of queer history. That was all blocked from us because our education assumed heterosexuality.

It impacted how I learned about sex. There was a "PG" way to have sex. Like, a socially acceptable way to have sex, to have relationships. But then there was a secret way that we had to make up between ourselves. Then the problems come when teenagers are trying to figure out sex, with a huge part of sex education missing. All the stuff about relationships, consent, identifying what makes you happy in all different relationships. I think that's a huge part of my life that I'm still catching up on, in a way.

Claire:
Mm-hmm. I have limited experience of what schools are like now. From what I know, there's more understanding. Especially when

it comes to relationships. Understanding each other, vulnerability, being open, communication, consent, talking. Well, that wasn't in our language. We had no idea about consent when we were growing up. Is that part of Section 28? Probably. Is that also to do with the wider curriculum of sex education? Definitely.

I mean, I'm sure kids today still have their challenges. One thing I am grateful for is not being at High School in the age of social media. Can you imagine?! I don't even want to go there. It would've been so, so much harder. I feel grateful in that regard. But I think kids today are given tools and resources that we didn't have access to. And has that affected us as adults? Definitely.

I loved the way you summed up Section 28. We were always, always fighting a bully. Cause that's how I felt, definitely. But actually, the bigger bully was this law that was enforced across our lives.

Any final thoughts you'd like to wrap up with?

Beth:
I don't think so. What about you?

Claire:
No. I feel really light, actually. I think this has been a great experience.

CHAPTER 6

The Unbearable Weight of Silence

BY HARRIS EDDIE HILL
(THEY/THEM)

Harris is a best-selling author, podcaster, neurodivergent and non-binary mental health coach. After years in the intersectional advocacy space, Harris is now directly supporting LGBTQIA+ and neurodivergent people to thrive via coaching, mentoring and story-telling.

Content Warnings
Suicide, Sex, Transphobia

PREFACE

At the time I'm writing this I'm 34, and have been out as trans non-binary for over 8 years. I attended a single-sex school from the late nineties, but at the time didn't know I was nonbinary, so have kept any references to gender as I understood them at the time. I have included several stories pertinent to the subject, but rest assured there were countless more examples that I have not.

I have gently made reference to suicide and sex, but have included no details, except for one childish sex-related rumour. Bullying, oppression and rejection, however, are more prominent throughout the piece.

I've also discovered as an adult that I'm neurodivergent, and for me this adds a layer of uncertainty and nervousness around etiquette that is not explicitly stated and explained, particularly during the time that this piece is set.

THE UNBEARABLE WEIGHT OF SILENCE

So much of what we learn about discrimination and bigotry is explicit; slurs, refusing people service, telling people their way of life is immoral, or even making an aspect of their identity illegal. So often we hear of stories in the media about children or young people who've been kicked out of their homes or excommunicated from their communities. Or perhaps the tragic stories of school children who've been so bullied, they felt that life wasn't worth living anymore.

I have heard examples like this a thousand times, and have quite a few of my own to add to the pile. But the part of oppression that doesn't share half of the spotlight, as I feel it should, is the way silence is used to oppress the marginalised. The fact that it remains nameless and unaddressed means it can permeate a culture like an odourless gas, gradually getting into people's bloodstreams without anyone noticing.

Like almost everyone my age I've spoken to about Section 28, I had never heard of it until now. Had you asked me before if I had ever felt oppressed or discriminated against, I'd have reeled off some examples of overt and explicit slurs, bullying, or rejection. But looking back, I feel like Section 28 and the ripple effect it had socially far outweighs all of those incidents combined. The way it insidiously informed our teachers' dampening comments, the school's silent permissiveness of the feral and unchecked homophobic bullying that spread like wildfire, it seems so obvious now. But at the time it just felt like one of those things we dealt with silently on our own.

As an early teen I was once skipping down the school corridor, hand-in-hand with one of my oldest friends, Hannah, only to be hissed at by our walking stereotype of a lesbian PE teacher, 'Girls! Stop doing that!'. Luckily my inherited wind-up gene, which I seemed to share in common with Hannah, kicked in before we allowed shame and oppression to get the better of us, and we continued to skip higher and laughed even louder. But there was a part of me still looking back, silently haunted by our teacher's attempt to both sexualise and oppress our behaviour. Although the undesired behaviour was never named and remained unspoken in that moment, Hannah and I both knew exactly why she'd told us to stop and had attempted to vomit her shame over us.

Home wasn't much different. Although I'd never been told explicitly that I wasn't to discuss queerness, any attempt to do so seemed unappreciated and made people uncomfortable. We had gay family friends, but I'd only been told around the age of ten, so it felt implicitly like information we didn't loudly share.

Unbeknownst to me, Section 28 had officially ended whilst I was doing my GCSEs, but there was no noticeable change in the unspoken rule of silence, as far as I was concerned. During that time I'd come to know a girl in the year above me, Kayleigh, who seemed so confident and cool. She was a rebel, but easy to laugh with and didn't seem to think anything of missing classes or deciding not to go to something that to me would have felt mandatory. I don't remember her ever saying anything unkind, but I do remember the days she didn't come in because she'd been hospitalised overnight from alcohol poisoning or similar.

As we began to hang out, there was something I started to feel. It wasn't the same feeling I felt with boys, because I was allowed, if not encouraged to do that. There was something secretive, yet also safe about the feeling with this older girl. She ultimately felt unattainable and fairly aloof, but perhaps that's what made it feel safe and helped me to feel easy about it?

At this point, had I had any adults to talk to about the situation, they might have warned me about the red flags. Or even made me aware of what to look for, or what behaviours were indicative of a more serious problem. But as it was, this was something I had to go through and work out by myself. I did have friends to talk to about what was going on, but they were often less experienced than I was when it came to dating.

One evening I found myself staying over at Kayleigh's for a sleep-over. I must have been about 14 or 15. I remember things had gone well throughout the evening, but by the time it got to the point where cuddling might have happened, she swiftly avoided the situation and put on a psychologically disturbing film, which completely ruined the moment and left me feeling certain that she'd changed her mind.

Back at school she was cooler towards me. When friends had asked what had happened and I told them, the consensus was that she'd bottled it. Which in our immature brains made no sense when she had the reputation of being a very carefree, fanny-loving lesbian. It was a complete mystery to us at the time, and I had no one with any experience to ask, unlike the times when I was dating boys and felt free to express my usual unfiltered self.

After a while she started paying attention to me again, which was extremely confusing. Then, in a larger gesture, she invited me to a friends' dinner in town one weekend, and even went so far as to declare it a 'date'. I accepted cautiously and hoped that perhaps she'd just been nervous the first time around.

We had dinner in a family-run and very popular Italian restaurant with her friends and some of their friends. I remember us disturbing the other diners with a drunken rendition of 'Take On Me'. As the drinks became more regular, however, I started to notice that Kayleigh had begun to talk more with the pink-haired girl next to her, Amy. Amy had been brought to dinner to cheer her up as she'd recently been thrown out of home and was living at the YMCA. It was never explicitly stated that she'd been thrown out for being queer, but I think it was implicitly understood by everyone there.

I watched as Kayleigh and Amy's conversation built a bubble of giddiness around just the two of them, the amount of eye contact becoming exclusive to each other, and the gentle touches exchanged more frequent. By the end of the meal, as we peeled out of the restaurant, Kayleigh and Amy were roaring with energy, arm in arm, and then eventually lip-locked. They even disappeared down the darkened high street to have a few moments alone. I think the implication was that they'd done more than snogging, especially given the 'wahey!' they received from the group upon their return.

I remained silent, unsure of whether this was bad behaviour on their part, or perhaps just a part of queer culture that I felt too inept to understand or deal with. Ultimately I felt lost and alone, unsure of the rules and aware of a burgeoning belief that this outcome was somehow down to my own cluelessness. I didn't even have a Disney reference to hark back to. How do you navigate something totally alien in the dark, with no-one to call out to?

After the second failed attempt at a date, I let things lie and didn't try it again with her. Kayleigh fumbled an apology to me some time afterwards, but I just wanted to forget the whole thing. More than any potential rejection I might have felt, my main shame was around the fact that I was a total novice and didn't know how to be queer. I knew how to interact with boys because I'd had heteronormativity burned into my retinas from birth. And any information about dating boys, at school or at home, was treated as a regular, mundane occurrence. Even if it meant being a subservient doormat, I at least felt comfortable that I knew how to be with boys. It was familiar, albeit frequently unenjoyable.

Around this time, my dad picked me up after school one day. As we left the school gates and joined the main road, we stopped at the traffic lights to let the pedestrians cross, and there walked Kayleigh.

"That's my friend, Kayleigh," I pointed out to my dad. He didn't respond. "She's a lesbian," I offered, testing the waters with a raised heart rate, but with absolutely no idea what his reaction might be.

He looked instantly irritated and choked on an attempted word, paused, and then spat, "why do I need to know that?"

I did not feel encouraged to say anything further, so we fell back to sitting in silence once more. It felt unnatural for me to be so secretive, but I didn't feel there was any other choice.

My next foray into queerdom was marginally more successful, but I couldn't have known how severe the consequences would be.

At a house party early that summer a large number of us gathered at David's family home. There were fellow students from our single-sex school as well as boys from the associated boys' school, and a handful of other students and older teenagers who'd left education already. One of the lads had recently come into the name Gherkin Rhys as he'd purportedly eaten a gherkin from his girlfriend's orifice (not her face). Whether this was true or not did not affect the glee that accompanied referring to him as Gherkin Rhys.

Several hours into the party, a queer girl called Corinne, who had a reputation for being liberally affectionate, struck up a conversation with me, and plied me with a couple of beers. We'd met many times previously, but this was the first instance of her chatting me up. She didn't go to our school, but she was friends with many of mine, and her intimidating cousin, Giulietta, also happened to be in my year.

After a couple of beers the sun had set, and she assertively took my hand and led me upstairs through the other partygoers. Finally.

It happened quietly in someone's bed, although I didn't know whose. There were a couple of people passed out on the floor. It was brief, awkward, and all conducted under the covers in the dark. I didn't dislike it, but it was strange and transactional, not to mention that we were unevenly matched; I being completely inexperienced and she clearly knowing what she was doing. If only sex education had covered this.

Once it was over, I must have fallen asleep. When I came to in the dim light of the early morning, I crept downstairs to see her quietly having sex with another girl on the living room sofa. I retreated so as not to disturb them and spent a while contemplating the meaning of what we'd done, and why she had already moved onto someone else whilst I was still there, at the very same party. I didn't know what to make of it and had no one to ask, so stayed silent on the matter.

I returned home quiet, feeling rejected and ashamed at yet another failed attempt to hold someone's attention for more than a matter of minutes. Surely by the second time I had to consider that I just wasn't interesting enough? Without anyone experienced to ask and share my doubts with, the shame began to fester.

Back at school, I was sat in a class next to Jane. She belonged to one of the two anti-social groups in our year, but like many of them, when she was on her own, was completely approachable and we got on fine. She was close to Corinne's cousin, Giulietta, so I made extra sure not to even mention the party. I hadn't shared what had happened with anyone besides maybe a close friend or two, and was too embarrassed at my potential failure to hold someone's interest for more than a brief fumble to make a big deal out of it. I had also reached the conclusion that I definitely was queer, but probably also too young to repeat the experience for now.

"I heard what happened at David's party," Jane said quietly.

I immediately blanched. The look on her face told me exactly what she knew, but I didn't confirm or deny it.

"You need to be careful. If Giulietta finds out, she's gonna go mental. I promise I won't tell her, but people are gossiping about it."

"How would anyone know?" I panicked. I knew the close friends I'd told would never break confidence, not to mention they had nothing to do with these groups at school; we all avoided them like the plague.

"Someone was asleep on the floor of the bedroom, apparently," Jane said.

It was only a matter of time before Giulietta found out and I was counting the days, waiting for the shoe to drop. One day, another one of her friends passed me in the bustling corridor and said 'Giulietta's looking for you'. I avoided responding and spent lunchtime for the next two weeks under Hannah's desk, hiding from her. Either Giulietta or one of her friends would swing open the classroom door abruptly most lunchtimes asking if anyone had seen me. I'd hold my breath under the table, mid-sandwich, and hear everyone deny my being there.

By the end of the second week I was a nervous wreck. At home, sat at the kitchen table, I burst into tears.

"What's wrong?" mum asked me. I met her eyes and considered telling her the truth. I really felt I was in trouble and that I didn't have the maturity to resolve the situation on my own, and knew intuitively that the teachers didn't approve of people like me. So I steeled myself with what little energy I had left and told her.

"I got off with someone at a party. Their cousin who goes to my school found out and is furious. She's been hunting me for two weeks."

"What was this boy's name?" asked mum.

"Her name was Corinne."

Mum paused. Then said, "I'm sure it's just a phase."

I paused, invalidated and equally frustrated by the irrelevance of her statement. "Well, I'm getting bullied now, anyway. I don't know what to do."

Mum told me that the best thing I could do was to go to school on Monday, go and find Giulietta, and confront her. It was not the response I was expecting, and the advice seemed completely mental. No mention of getting the school involved, no mention of talking to a teacher. Just go up to the person who's been threatening you and let whatever is going to happen, happen. Had this been bullying of any other kind, parents and teachers were usually involved until the matter was settled. Not this time.

It seemed like a massive gamble, and I felt hugely unprotected, but it was the only advice from an adult I had and I wasn't prepared to confide in anyone else. So on Monday lunchtime, with the entire group of my friends who'd been harbouring me under their desks for two weeks behind me, we stood outside Giulietta's form room and waited for her to come out.

"I heard you wanted to speak to me?" I asked calmly, whilst inside thinking I was likely to throw up.

"Yeah, I heard you shagged my cousin at that party. It's fucking disgusting."

"Well, it's really none of your business." I stated. "What do you want?"

"I want you to stay the fuck away from my cousin."

"She pursued me, so why don't you tell her that?"

"How could you do it? It's disgusting."

"Well if you don't like it, don't have gay sex. Are we done?"

"Yeah we're done."

And that was that. Luckily for my nerdy friends and I, no physical intervention was needed as I'm not sure many of us would have been up to the task. But I did feel backed up having them all stand behind me whilst there was only one of her.

I look back now and think about how much more pain and suffering came from broken silence and secrets coming out, given that secrecy was the only protection available. Thank god for my friends and their unwavering convictions. I didn't have the headspace at the time to consciously appreciate their allyship, but looking back I couldn't have asked for better.

I had initially felt safe exploring my romantic feelings and sexuality, knowing that it was private and not spoken about. But my private business being aired had resulted in a pressured coming-out to and risky advice from my mum, accompanied by invalidation, and simultaneously finding my 15-year-old self without any hint of backup from school. There was something slightly *Lord of the Flies* about it. Only we weren't stranded on an island alone; we were legally prevented from being protected, surrounded by adults who were responsible for us, but whose hands were either tied, or they were indifferent, or worse, they were traitors like the lesbian PE teacher.

Silence left me without safety, it left me without the words to express what I was going through, and it deprived me of any joy that I might have had the opportunity to experience, but never got to. Silence made finding community difficult. It made navigating the trauma and cluelessness within what little community I did have impossible. It made me believe that the rare few of my community I'd managed to find either didn't like me, or that I didn't fit in there either, or that everyone was too damaged to ever be happy.

I watch my friends' kids now talk so openly about their queer identities. Some of them have these sweet and innocent queer relationships in their first years at secondary school. I see their parents, my friends, delight in the beautiful innocence of these once-forbidden connections. I see the easiness with which those kids navigate their relationships, just as their straight peers do. I notice their indifference to queer characters on TV because they've seen so much of it already that it's normal to them. It contrasts so bitter-sweetly to my heart-wrenching joy that I still experience to this day, watching the same things, unsure if I'll ever be able to take it for granted, having suffered through the dark absence of it.

I hope they'll never know. I hope we're the last children to ever have to live through such a thing.

CHAPTER 7

Superman Was My Beard

BY ELISE LENNOX
(SHE/HER)

Elise Lennox is a queer writer from Glasgow.

Content Warnings
Homophobia, Bullying

Everyone had their 'thing' in primary school. A sport, TV show, franchise or celebrity they were obsessed with, knew everything about. Posters on the wall, branded pencil cases, sticker books, the works.

My thing was Superman. More specifically, the hit 90s show *Lois and Clark: The New Adventures of Superman.* I had posters, I had a scrapbook with pictures of the cast, I rose at 8am every Saturday morning to watch repeats before *Live and Kicking.*

I wasn't particularly bothered about 'Superman' as a concept or franchise – who cared about the comics or the Christopher Reeve films? No, my obsession was exclusive to that particular show.

Everyone in school knew that Superman was my thing, that I was obsessed. "Ooh, Dean Cain!" they'd simper, imagining that I was drawn to his Lycra-clad muscles and smouldering superhero grin.

In actual fact, Superman was my beard.

Sure, I had posters of Dean Cain on my wall, but only because he was standing next to the real object of my affections: Teri Hatcher. Teri Hatcher wrapped in a red cloak, winking, with that Lois Lane shiny brown bob. Teri Hatcher in a skimpy white tank top with a mock Superman tattoo on her bicep. Teri Hatcher in a 90s business suit. Be still, my faster-than-a-speeding-bullet heart. I don't think I glanced once at Superman's tight suit – the woman next to him was always so much more alluring.

Of course, an obsession with Dean Cain was a very useful cover for my Sapphic inclinations. Yes, I confirmed: Yes, I love Superman. Yes, isn't Dean Cain "hot". Whatever.

I can only imagine how much more mis-spent my youth would have been, had the internet and social media existed in the 90s. Back then you had to work for your obsession – you couldn't just type 'Teri Hatcher' into a search engine or follow her on Instagram and see every delectable picture of her ever taken. No, I had to take what I could find, leafing through endless magazines and newspapers to find clippings, interviews, pictures. On one embarrassing occasion I had to explain to my aunt why I, a 12-year-old girl, wanted to cut a picture of an actress wearing a skimpy black nightie out of her TV magazine. (I still have that picture and it is still a thing of beauty).

I couldn't have cared less what any Superman looked like in his red and blue onesie, how long he had to spend in the gym to get those muscles. Give me a karate-chopping, no-nonsense Lois Lane with hair shinier than the sun any day.

Fast forward to the early 2000s and I find myself in the same situation with Sunday-evening family drama *Monarch of the Glen*. Another supposedly hunky actor, this time playing a Highland laird: another of my TV beards. It was so easy to imply to schoolfriends and family members that Archie, Laird of Glenbogle, was the reason for my obsession with the show, the reason I watched every episode and then went out and bought the DVDs. In fact, it was another dazzling brunette who had caught my eye – the cheeky housekeeper Lexie, played by Dawn Steele. Lexie wearing a bikini top to do the housework, Lexie going fishing in a miniskirt and welly boots. Hoots mon.

Indeed, Sunday evening TV was a treasure trove for a young queer girl: before Lexie lit up the Highlands, the intrepid crew of *Star Trek: Voyager* would fight another Klingon... or whatever.

Again, I wasn't hugely interested in the plot or franchise, yet I watched the show religiously, entranced by the addition of a new crew member: Seven of Nine. Who could possibly look twice at any male superhero in a Lycra suit after seeing Seven of Nine? Has anyone ever worn Borg implants so well? Unfortunately, a lot of middle-aged men seemed to share my opinion, which made me feel incredibly disgusted with myself. Was I comparable to those leering creeps who joked that the addition of Seven of Nine to the cast was 'something for the Dads'?

How could I know? Scottish education under Section 28 was not conducive to discovering that my feelings were normal, that there was nothing wrong with me. The first time I heard the word 'lesbian', at the age of about 10, it was portrayed as a disgusting thing; a terrible affliction. I went home from school and curled up in my bedroom, terrified that I was like that – it was the first time I'd ever heard a word that described how I felt and it was very clearly a bad and shameful thing to be.

I gradually convinced myself that I couldn't possibly be a lesbian because I didn't find boys repulsive. There must be some other word, I thought, so many years away from discovering that bisexuality was a thing. I may not have known what I was, but at least I could tell myself I wasn't that awful word.

For at least the first 10 years of my life I assumed that everyone found their own gender attractive and that men and woman marrying each other was a kind of administrative task that had to be carried out in order to have a family. At the same time, I realised that this wasn't something to be discussed – I had never have seen any positive representations of non-heterosexual relationships in any kind of media. This is why I find the idea of Section 28 and today's continued pearl-clutching about LGBTQIA+ – particularly the T – education so baffling.

Everyone has their own journey, but a huge number of people know that they are queer from a very early age, before they can even vocalise or describe their feelings. I certainly did – I would never have said it out loud and didn't know that there were words for it, but I cannot remember a time in my life when I didn't know that I found women attractive.

The only thing that Section 28 did for me was to convince me that there was something wrong with me and to force me to push down and hide a huge part of myself away for decades. Even now I have residual shame about the way I am and don't feel able to be fully out to everyone I know.

Had I learnt about non-heterosexual relationships in school, it would not have 'turned' me gay – that's not possible. However, I would have known that I was not abnormal, that I didn't need to feel a deep and burning shame about myself. On many mornings, I felt disgusted going into school, knowing that other girls wouldn't want to be friends with me or be near me if they knew how I felt inside. It was even worse when changing rooms or – shock, horror – shared rooms on school trips were involved. I'm sure I gave myself a few headaches from staring intently at my own gym bag or pillow to avoid even glancing at any other girl in the room, lest she accuse me of 'perving' on her.

On several occasions, friends commented that I was aloof and questioned why I never hugged them or got changed in front of them them. What was I to say? That I was worried that if I did these things and they then discovered I was queer, they would accuse me of fancying them? One girl in particular that I had a huge crush on throughout sixth year commented after we left school that she thought she had done something to offend me as I avoided being in close proximity to her so studiously.

I have no doubt that there were others in my year group at school going through the same thing – at least two boys I was friendly with came out almost as soon as they left school. Is that why we were such good friends, I wondered, feeling despair that they couldn't have come out in that environment.

Even when I went to university, I felt too ashamed to go to any LGBTQIA+ meetups – I assumed that I wouldn't be queer enough, that they would criticise me for not being out or for not fully knowing who I was. I wish I could go back in time and do it differently – I know that, had I taken that step, I would probably have met people who would have helped and supported me. Unfortunately, the few people I did come out to, when I identified as bisexual, had uniformly negative reactions.

From straight people, variations on a theme of: 'it's a phase, you're just looking for attention, you're trying to attract men by suggesting you'll have a threesome.'

From several queer people, variations on a theme of: 'it's a stepping stone to lesbianism, you're just experimenting, you'll come over to our side eventually.'

I was in my thirties before I had what I call my 'les-piphany'. Having since re-evaluated my earlier feelings and ideas about identity, I can trace the absolute certainty I had in my teens and twenties that I was NOT a lesbian to those early negative connotations. I spent almost two decades convincing myself that bisexuality was a more acceptable identity than full-blown lesbianism, only to have my entire sexual identity laid clear in a thunderbolt-like moment of clarity.

I was having a conversation in a professional capacity about a story I had written in which the main characters were lesbians. The person I was talking to raised the issue of representation; whether there would be questions over my right as a 'straight woman' to write queer characters. Shit, I thought, here I am having to come out again. My mouth started to say "actually, I'm bisexual," but stopped. Suddenly, with absolute clarity, I knew that I was not bisexual. I knew, in that second, that I was, and always had been, a lesbian.

Of course, mid-conversation with a colleague is not the ideal time to have any kind of existential Sapphic crisis. I stumbled and, with hideous awkwardness, came out with one of the most embarrassing sentences of my life: "actually... I'm... erm... I'm... not straight."

Not straight. Technically true, but only the starting point of a long conversation I would go on to have with myself over the following months.

I occasionally drive past my old high school, which now has a large Pride flag flying outside the main entrance. How different would my own process of self-acceptance and self-understanding have been had that flag flown so proudly in the mid-2000s, had I been able to walk past a visual symbol of tolerance every morning?

I certainly would not still be half closeted in my mid-30s, still struggling with how to be honest about myself and those around me.

One thing at least has changed for the better: the wall next to my desk is now adorned with posters featuring actors from Carol, Desert Hearts and Gentleman Jack. Beautiful and inspirational women, with no men – not even Supermen – to dull their shine and lend them a heteronormative respectability.

I may have some way to go in my journey to full out-and-proud queerness, but at least I have shaved off my beard.

CHAPTER 8

Born Criminal

BY DALTON HARRISON
(HE/HIM)

Dalton Harrison is a transgender man who writes poetry about his experience of transition and prison in the hope it will help others. He is currently studying criminal justice and criminology at University.

Content Warnings
Bullying, Violence, Homophobia, Transphobia

You gave me a name,
Frame me in words passed down,
Loudly almost proudly that social stability
can only be found in notions constructed
and forged by the fire of preconceived devotions,

Centuries of Laws and punishments,
Section 28 is just an echo in all this commotion,

I sit in the smoking shell of my body,
In the aftermath of an empty bullet chamber,
That was once used to kill those who looked like me,
I hold my sweaty hands together
as if the very act of prayer might save me,

Yet it's the whispered prayer under breath condoned by history,
That carry-on the reason society sees,
a sin as a sin,
I crumble under police boots,

Each print marks my face,
Yet I am a child,
Sat in a classroom learning about morality,
Yet all I see,

Is you telling me,
I mean nothing,
I am neither blood nor bone,
Protest signs or bricks,

My house is made of hay and sticks,
I sit holding my breath trying to beat death,

I am a child growing up already feeling like a criminal,
Till one day I am.

Yet this cell feels no different
than the body you tell me I have to live with,
I am no longer a child,
I am a generation marked out in history,
Where violence was ok if you did not fit in,

Where bruises were hidden because no one saved the voiceless,
I could quote you the Bible but where has that got me,
I am still fighting,
There are more wars than triumphs,

I am a generation who relives the taste of salt and blood-red lips,
I am more than my mistakes,
You can count on this,
But I haven't forgotten those who died to get me here,

I haven't forgotten the system that tells us not to corrupt the kids,
Yet what was replaced after section 28?
No evolution only the conclusion,
society still deems me a criminal.

CHAPTER 9

Problem Child

BY PHOEBE GREEN
(SHE/HER)

Phoebe Green is a researcher from Manchester.

Content Warnings
Homophobia, Bullying

When people talk about gay culture, they often talk about gay men as if lesbians don't exist. If often feels like there are so many stereotypes, like lesbians are either cock-teasers or they just don't want to be hit on tonight. Lesbians shouldn't exist because, if they're not there for men, what's the point of them?

I was at secondary school in the 1990s and I knew I was gay from about the age of seven. I'd always assumed that at some point it would sort itself out, because that's what we were told, you know – "it's not right, but when you become a teenager it will all sort itself out and you'll start finding men attractive, it just happens."

I confided in a friend at school, and the next thing I know, everyone knew. It was the grapevine at work. So I spent all of secondary school being bullied for being the gay kid, and of course I was at an all-girls school, which probably didn't help matters. There were 120 girls in the year, how many must be in the LGBTQIA+ community? I can't have been the only one, but I was the only one who'd been stupid enough to tell someone.

I ended up being bullied quite badly for it, by people who didn't even know me, and it got to a point where one of my friends got dragged into it. She was straight, but she was bullied for being gay as well because she was friends with me. Her mum complained to the school, and we all got hauled into a little cupboard with some of the people who were bullying, and we all had this sit-down conversation. I did not raise my voice at all in this. Her mum had complained, I didn't know what was going on.

They were very careful not to touch on what it was, because obviously Section 28 was still in force, so they couldn't talk about it. It was all about "so you're doing the bullying", they never asked why – they never asked what the reason was, and every time it looked like it was going to come up, they would smother it so fast.

At the end of the meeting, they said, "Everyone out of the room!" and held me back, even though I was not involved in raising the issue. I was just like, "yeah, they've done some shit." And they were like, "It sounds like they're giving you a really hard time," and I said, "I guess so," because I'd kind of got used to it by that point.

I just ploughed on. And they said, "well, we have someone who comes in to deal with some of the problem students, and usually it's because they're too aggressive, but in your case it sounds like you might not be aggressive enough!" So they were basically trying to get me lumped in as a problem student. I wasn't even the one who had raised it, but they knew I was the problem, because at that point, I was seen as a problem.

So rather than tackling the bullies, and saying, "You shouldn't be bullying anyone, for any reason" – you can do that without talking about why they're bullying, just "don't be a dick!" But they made it my problem, my fault. I had to do that in order to stop them being tarnished as bullies.

This was section 28. This is how it impacted me - I was seen as the problem, not the victim. It was a really shit time, because everyone seemed to hate gay people, but nobody at school was really old enough to understand why. No-one knew why they hated each other, no-one knew why they were being mean to me, but they just knew that I wasn't acceptable. It was a horrible time to be gay.

I left in 2002, a year before Section 28 was repealed. It was in place throughout my entire time in education.

I found one of my old school reports recently, and it was really interesting to read. It would say things that implied "your child has depression, please do something about it!" but they didn't use those words, and they certainly couldn't say what it was that was making me depressed in the first place.

When it came to choosing prefects and things I was completely overlooked, because obviously they can't put me in a position – they can't be seen to endorse me in any way. I was a high flyer, but I went through secondary school feeling unseen, because every time I stuck my head above the parapet I was shot down. Tt was because of who I was, rather than because of anything I did, and that hurt.

I look back on Section 28 and think it was one of the worst things the world has done to LGBTQIA+ people. I know it's probably not, but because I lived through it – because it silenced us - it still feels so raw.

When you take someone's voice away, they've got nothing.

CHAPTER 10

My Inalienable Right to be Gay

BY KIT GEE
(THEY/THEM)

Kit Gee is a poet, performance writer and an artistic collaborator with Berlin-based performance collective Once We Were Islands.

Content Warnings
Homophobia, Conservative Evangelical Christianity, Medical Transphobia, Shame, Deliberate Outing, CSA

PREFACE

Section 28 was many things including a silencing. I have chosen speech as a medium of response to this silencing and have constructed this essay from transcripts of conversations, performance and micro-performance which I have conducted as a basis for the text that follows.

Acknowledgements
Thank you to L, who was there at the time.
Thank you to E, who wasn't.
Thank you to nameless other people who listened.
Thank you to nameless other people who were not silent - then and now.

This piece is both chronological and conversational. The breaks in the storytelling are present-day discussion around the theme.

MY AC(COUNT)

Evening. Thank you all for coming to hear my ac(count). Thank you, Lois Weaver, for teaching me how to do some of this. Thank you, Joe Brainard, for teaching me how to do the rest. Okay...? Okay. Okay, buckle up.

I'm 41. I'm standing in front of you, wondering what it will be like to tell you all this.

I'm 1, I'm 2, I'm 3. And I'm not a girl and I'm not a boy and I'm noticing this fact isn't going down very well at home.

I'm 4. Tiny people march in grainy longshot across the TV screen. Some are miners. Some are... not miners? Something else? There is a vibe in the room. I march my toys around, again and again. I am not allowed to do this in front of my grandmother. I do this in front of my grandmother. There is another vibe in the room.

I'm 5. I have one particular dolly, called Katherine, who I am struggling to connect with. I feel guilty about it. I make great efforts to include her, but our relationship is blocked. I consider telling Blossom, my other dolly, how I feel but I don't want to burden Blossom or impact any relationship Blossom and Katherine might be having outside of my involvement.

I'm awake at night replaying in my mind the television sequence of a tombstone crunching to the floor. 'AIDS: Don't Die of Ignorance'. I feel very implicated. What does any of this mean? Richard - the most feminine child in my class, including the girls - and I are committed partners for Country Dancing. We've swapped sides; Richard dances the girls' steps and I dance the boys' steps. This feels fun. This feels serious. This is serious fun.

I am 6. A woman in blue on the telly. 'Prime Minister'. 'Oh'. Blue background. Lots of blue going on. Earrings. "Children who need to be taught to respect traditional moral values are being taught that they have an inalienable right to be gay. All of those children are being cheated of a sound start in life. Yes, cheated" I'm having a confusing response to these words - panic? No idea why. In the middle, a kind of clarity - my dolly, Katherine, looks the spit of Maggie Thatcher. I can't unsee it. I don't want to hug Maggie Thatcher. I don't want Maggie Thatcher in my bedroom.

I'm 7. Section 28 comes into force but I don't know that yet. I'm hearing the word 'homosexual' a lot, though. At church. No silencing going on there. I heard this word once before at a dinner round at my parents' friends' house. Hmmm. So... some people are not homosexual? Huh. So... there's a word for me. But it's... bad?

I'm 8. Two men kiss on *EastEnders* but their happiness, and mine, is short-lived. I'm in front of a doctor because I'm not a girl. The doctor tells me that I will never be loved. Mum cries, her view confirmed.

I'm 9. I'm 10. With no evidence to the contrary, being gay is bad even though it is one of the things I love best about me. So...I'm bad. I'm going to get killed by a falling tombstone. "That won't happen to you"- Why?-"because you're a girl" I'm not a girl, I'm going to get killed by a falling tombstone and I will - apparently - richly deserve it. I can't repent of my gayness because God will know I'm lying through my teeth.

I'm 11. First week of secondary school. A girls' school. Draw a portrait of yourself when you are old. I love Art and I love this task. Mine is the only one that doesn't go up on the wall display. There must have been a mistake.

"No, no mistake". The teacher thrusts the portrait back at me. I don't understand. I walk along the corridor holding my portrait. An older student stops me. "Wow", she says, "Did you do this? Do you know the man you've painted, or did you make him up?"

I faint in a sex education lesson in the Science department. This hilarious incident will be chuckled over in front of me by staff and students alike for the next 7 years - taken as evidence of me being weak and cossetted and squeamish. I faint in that Science lesson because I realise that I have been subject to sexual abuse over a number of years. Another thing that can't be spoken about. Nothing important can be. Silence is harmful to me but I don't have a voice, and even if I did have a voice I don't have any words, and even if I did have words I am schooled in shame.

I know - from all the compounding silences - that there is absolutely nobody else like me and that concurrently- confusingly- everyone like me is bad and deserves what they get. Also, PS- God rejects me because I am not, after all, a virgin. PPS- Despite the insistence of a brutal array of children in the school corridors, I'm also not a lesbian. I think explaining that I'm not a girl will clear the matter up but - bafflingly, as this is all surely just a simple case of mistaken identity - it doesn't. Now I'm a fucking queer faggot, too. Oh.

I'm 12. Puberty is ruining all of my closest relationships. ALL. OF. THEM. I have gay role models - all except 2 being Bible characters. Ruth and Naomi - 'Wherever you go, I will go'; Jacob who defied gender norms and became the father of the 12 tribes of Israel; Jonathan, who made a covenant with David, 'because he loved him as his own soul'. Are the preachers and I even reading the same book?

I am 13. Oh. Pants. It has just occurred to me that I've been congratulating myself on being holy and pure, but the truth is I'm just very much not sexually attracted to teenage boys. Like, at all. I am especially not attracted to the ones who are attracted to me. Of which there are mercifully few. I love moving through the world as a teenage boy; I'm very much attracted to that, and I can do it with ease but I spend a year not being in contact with my joy and instead actively pretending to be 'normal'. Whatever 'normal' is, I am unsuccessful at portraying it. Nobody is convinced and I am more miserable than ever.

I'm 14. I'm in a classroom, a cover lesson, not our usual teacher. A single sentence mention of homosexuals in a textbook about the Holocaust; I'm stunned. There is a 'debate' about homosexuality. A lull. Nobody is saying anything now. I'm very queer although I haven't yet reclaimed that term.

There is no way that the teacher in this room is straight. I have gaydar now! This is so horrific. I need the silence in the room to break. I stand up and start talking. I deftly outline all the reasons that I've heard through my whole life about why being gay is wrong. Sources for this are: pulpit speakers at my church, unchallenged homophobic bullies at school, the princely two narrative arcs involving a gay person in televised dramas that I've seen, news reports.

As I talk, I am mentally marshalling all the counterevidence I have to show why that is wrong... but... I've never articulated any of this counterevidence before... and... these don't yet have a vocabulary... I have no words to hang these passions on.. and so.. no words... come.....out. What are these strange noises that I can hear? Oh, I am making these noises. They are noises, they are not yet words. Humiliation. I'm the queerest person I know and I have- apparently- just made a persuasive case for the intrinsic wrongness of gayness. The silence seems to stretch and stretch. Now some people are clapping. I can't bring myself to yield the floor. What has just happened?

I'm 15. I've become politicised over the summer after witnessing police violence. I'm actively campaigning for equal marriage. I'm officially unlovable and - luckily, I guess, in light of this - I also don't want to get married. I can only answer questions with questions. 'Why is this cause so important to you?' Because...Because... JUST BECAUSE! 'Why ISN'T it important to YOU?!', I want to yell. An answer, of sorts, although not really. I'm attracted to a teenage boy! Although only, apparently, if he is wearing his ecclesiastical vestments and more particularly if he is also wearing eyeliner. What to make of this?

I am 16. I meet L. One of my new teachers.

K: "Hello."

L: "Hello."

K: "The reason we're having a chat is because I remember a conversation with you some years ago where we were talking about T___ and you said that was your impression that it was a forward thinking, progressive and inclusive school and that was not at all my recollection. And so, I just wondered, do you still feel that now?"

L: "No, I don't think that now."

K: "For me, it's really important to sort of try to understand it. Like, in the context of history. I'm like, you know, there it it may well have been a massively progressive space for the time.

I don't know. I've only got a kind of a child's perspective, I suppose, on what it felt like for me. But I, you know, I can well believe that for the context of the time and for the area that we were in, it might well have been like a shining beacon of inclusion."

L: "I think I don't think we can say that, can we? I don't think we can say it was that. I think I think the very most that we could say was that for me it felt like a more accepting space than any that I'd previously experienced.

But that is coming from a perspective of somebody
kind of outside that community looking in and looking
on and not knowing, you know?"

I'm still 16. I leave compulsory education with no relevant
sexual health education and no knowledge of consent. I'm starting
Sixth Form.

Now I'm 17. I'm still in Sixth Form. I've been working in
Theatre; so this is where all the gay people have been all along.
I'm going through a messy break-up with Conservative Evangelical
Christianity.

I'm 18. I don't get into uni. Fortitude. Fortitude. I'm not at
school anymore and I'm trying to make sense of some of my school
experiences retrospectively. I'm getting very het-up about Section
28; all roads seem to be leading me to this piece of legislation. It has
to go. People are being harmed. Not me, obviously; 'people'. I'm a
queer, I'm not a full person. Oh, hang on... ermmm.

I am 19. And I'm at uni! I'm gay-bashed for the first time
and two passing policemen join in! I'm still going through a messy
break-up with Conservative Evangelical Christianity but with the
added bonus of being denounced from the pulpit and the extra
added bonus of not living in the same place as that particular pulpit
anymore.

I do need to repent, but not in church, and not to that crowd.
I'm going out in Soho, having religious experiences on dancefloors,

splitting my evenings after shows between the clubs and the one-person street ministry I've spontaneously started. I've seen Peter Tatchell in action - is he an escapee, too? I have no actual idea but I know what I'm seeing and I've got skills thanks to my thorough Evangelical training- I take to the streets to apologise, take responsibility, and to listen and learn, and to hold space for angry and hurt queer people of faith and of no faith.

People like me. I'm expecting to hear stories about the church, and I do, and I hear about families and doctors and I hear about schools and schools, schools, schools. Scotland have done it; our turn next. Section 28 out!

L: "It wasn't enough. In schools, I mean. It wasn't celebratory, we know that now."

K: "I think like I I feel like it's OK for us to be forgiving to our younger selves because we were young. You were young, I was young. It's quite interesting to hear you talk about kind of.the way that you've sort of become sensitised to these issues over time."

L: "It's personal now. It matters to me massively... That would make... that would make it- wouldn't it?- for everybody, if if it were just personal."

I'm 20. I'm angry. I'm on a stage. I'm trying to explain to a crowd of students why a largely symbolic law, under which there have been no successful prosecutions, should be removed from the statute books and why this is urgent. URGENT! I'm trying to talk about the insidious nature of self-policing by individuals and institutions that Section 28 has inspired, and of the perils of the slippery wording of the bill. I'm largely unsuccessful.

Too abstract. Still too unable to name my experience. I'm using the word 'panopticon' instead of trying to say what Section 28 has done to me and to people I know. Not brave enough to tell the listening crowd what Section 28 has done to them, gay or not. I'm not connecting. 'Why is this cause important to you?'

That question again. Inside, I am Marsha P. Johnson changing the world; outside, I am a baby-faced weirdo with activism that is being read even by some close friends as an 'unintelligibly quirky hobby'. I can't really say exactly why this cause is important to me because I don't feel safe enough to really think about it and I don't want to cry. Ever. In front of anyone. Ever. Especially not here. For reasons that elude me, I have an adult baptism in to the Evangelical Christian Church and (immediately) never return to an Evangelical church again.

I'm clearly not okay.

I am 21. I'm working in burlesque doing gender-bending performance, and have a secret life in which I perform and socialise as Scott Free. Sometimes Scott Free works as a female impersonator called Maiden Voyage. I haven't asked myself any questions about why this part of my life is a secret or why this secret part feels the most real. Scott Free is me and is not me and is me and is Maiden Voyage who is me and is not me and is me and is Scott Free who is not me and who is me and is her and is not her. Scott Free is more popular than I am.

I'm 22. Section 28 is overturned in Westminster, to seemingly *zero* Press attention. I find one miniscule segment in The Guardian. More bloody silence. I don't know what to feel and these curly fries aren't cutting it.

K: "Getting Section 28 repealed was a lot of what I did – obviously not on my own!- at uni. I started campaigning actively for that before I went to uni and I went to uni in the year 2000 and that was the year that it was repealed in Scotland and then it was 2003 this side of the border.

Well, that was my whole B.A. 3 years, you know, basically. I vaguely remember Kent made their own local version, and that continued until 2010, when it subsequently contravened the Equality Act.

I'm pretty sure I am not making this up, but it sounds implausible as I say it out loud. I should fact-check it. I was kind of doing I guess like being quite actively engaged in that happening and also like being really aware even then that it still felt like I didn't have a clear view on it.

And and I guess I would count that now as still being quite young and and and damaged by it all."

I am 23. I'm 24.

K: "I remember Section 28 being introduced. I remember news reports. I remember listening to Margaret Thatcher saying that people - children?- falsely believe they have an inalienable right to be gay.

I remember thinking that feels really relevant to me, but I don't know why. Yeah, and also I remember her talk, like, lots of news clips of her talking about 'pretended family relationships'.

So I remember that that coming in and. and and finding it hard to like, grapple with why that quite that bothered me. And also that, that this - I couldn't, I wasn't able to draw the line between these things on the telly and my experience of actually being in school until I had left school. Uh, but you did your teacher training...uhh.. When did you do your teacher training?"

L: "'91, '92."

K: "Yes. So this was something that was so firmly established, Section 28, by then, I guess, if you look at the dates. So, what was teacher training...erm"

L: "It didn't come up. It didn't come up. Not mentioned."

K: "Right, so. Woah. That's really interesting, isn't it? So, I guess I'm sort of drawing parallels there now between my experiences - as a student - of erasure and silence.

And actually, I think what I'm hearing is that there's something - there was a sort of silencing around that for the teachers-in-training, too?"

L: "I mean teacher training has changed- who does it and where it happens is changed beyond measure. But at that time, it was very much in the hands of the of the kind of... Liberals. So, I have the sense that they weren't, that they would have not engaged with it."

K: "Ah, OK. So it's a sidestep."

L: "Yes, they would have sidestepped it. I think they would not have actively chosen to inculcate... with the... But I guess equally they were not... They did nothing to...

They were not at liberty to speak against it, but they also didn't want to endorse it. But you know, I suppose kind of retrospectively all the things that you think about now that would be... There was nothing..."

K: "...positive?"

L: "Positive effort, you know what I mean? You know that's kind of what we're saying, isn't it? That actually what to me in the '90s felt progressive was just a lack of negativity and and that's sad.

That's the sad thing to say, isn't it? It's a sad thing to say, but that was, you know, for me that was...That was progressive then because my own experience of it had been that there were all kinds of negativity around that in the school community. Hmm."

K: "Yeah."

L: "For me, you know, at the time I would be quite excited about something very small and that to me now looks like so, so little and so inadequate, if that makes sense."

K: "So much. This has. You've just. The idea of silence as a kindness is... I've never. I wasn't reading the Section 28 silence as a kind one."

I'm 25, 26, and 27. I'm working in schools. Wearing a wedding ring, photos of spouse and children on the desk, marriage certificate framed on her wall, a woman tells me that my personal life has no place in a school and should remain unspoken at work.

I am 28. I'm 29. I'm in a gay club and bump in to one of the policemen who joined in when he saw me being gay-bashed outside here 10 years ago. He is here with his husband. I go over to talk to him, wanting an apology, I think. I don't get an apology but I do get something more complicated - a long conversation in which the phrase 'new moral climate' is frequently repeated. Not by me. Section 28 is referenced. Again, not by me.

K: "I was involved with the outing of a political figure, and I wouldn't... I wouldn't do that now.

Because I'm older, I guess, and I think about it differently, for reasons that will become clear, but at the time there was this guy, he was a politician and he was extremely outspoken against gay people suddenly and I was bumping into him at gay clubs and it really, really fucked me off, and he - and just the kind of hypocrisy of that was completely unpalatable to me and also not just me, and as his sort of public rhetoric became even more staunch I felt like it made complete sense to be involved in the scheme at the time. So that happened.

And I - really very incorrectly - thought that that would matter and would alleviate oppression.

And basically, what happened was that it made my life worse, and it made the lives of lots of people in my community worse, and it made his life worse. Because what I hadn't understood was like public cultural perception of what was happening was very, very different to my experience as an individual person who would be buying a drink and having to see this man who was like actively endangering 'my people' as I felt and like not be able to hold that as a young person, I couldn't hold it.

I can't get my head around it that he was gay and going after gays and gay spaces also revelling in and being safe in those same gay spaces. How could this be? But what transpired was that the hypocrisy of this person, as we saw it, was not what was understood by the Press to be the issue and what was broadcast as his 'shame' was the fact of his gayness. That he was gay, full stop.

Which is the last thing that anyone should be made to feel ashamed of. And I and I, I guess like. that was like a massive wake-up, really, about; 'Ohh... actually there's this whole extra thing, which is public opinion and.it is what people more remote from the issue tap into, to make their individual opinions'. Do you know what I mean? Hmm, so I'm kind of, I feel like I'm sort of monologuing a bit here now...yeah...Not my finest hour."

I'm 30, 31, and 32. I'm working at a school where I can bring all the bits of my identity to work. These bits are celebrated, valued and at the same time very run-of-the-mill. I love it. I love it and I love it and I am having a confrontation with myself. Seeing the shape of me, held in contortion, bits guarded, twisted. It is unnecessary to expend energy holding this shape now, but I'm vigilant, I can't relax. I've been praised for my courage in activism but I have never had to be this consistently brave before. 'Equality Act 2010, Equality Act 2010', I repeat to myself as I walk along school corridors that smell the same as all school corridors before or since. I'm being asked to trust that I have solid ground underneath my feet and I don't know how to walk on something I don't fully believe in.

I'm 33. Another June, another Pride Assembly. High quality, high production values. As usual, the stage is invaded during the finale by the audience of young people and staff and we all dance together. This is what my teenage self needed and now, after a period of some delay, it gets it. Legacy of Section 28, fuck you! There is nothing left of you! There is only this moment of love and acceptance and celebration and visibility, and all the cosmic reverberations of this across time and space.

I'm 34. Oh. Different school. Cosmic reverberation bypass. Shit.

L: "I think probably, probably what I was bringing to that was like my own. So this, that was like my second teaching job after like my own, you know, I mean my own school experience was... I don't think there was anybody at my school that was openly gay and would tell you that.

I think that was, that was just, that was just not a thing. So I think where I was coming from and what I said to you is that when we were at T___, what I had the sense of is that there were people there who were openly gay and happy to say that, and happy to talk about that which to me was quite revolutionary, but that's coming from like a very conservative heterosexual perspective, and it was very different to the first school I taught at which was another girls' school in the very similar area, but didn't have that kind of attitude.

And so at T_____ that was my perspective. And then now I don't know how much of that was that that was an open thing? Or I just happened to notice? Do you know what I mean? I think it was that."

I'm 35. I'm 36.

K: "What do you feel is kind of different as a teacher in school spaces now? And do you connect that with the repeal of Section 28? Or do you feel like it's coming from other places?"

L: "Hmm. For a lot of years, Clause 28 was repealed, but it felt like the behaviours associated with that were rooted in education, and I think, you know, I agree, even now there is a sense of being careful. You need to be careful what you say and and I think that that comes in some ways from Clause 28. I think it can be it's like a kind of cultural hangover, if you like from that. I also think it is associated also with that kind of weird space that you occupy as a teacher in relation to in loco parentis kind of thing."

K: "Yeah, I would agree."

L: "You've got that responsibility to a young person of hearing what they say and being open to that and offering them a perspective on the world that is maybe different from the perspective that they have at home and being kind of open to that and making it clear that those things are all OK, but there's also that kind of - it's very easy to find yourself in a difficult situation with, with parents, you know, and I mean, you only need to go back to our personal experience. I think your mum wasn't my biggest fan."

K: "She wasn't. I don't think that was purely about my gender and sexuality, though. You were a voice in my ear that was entirely different to hers. On lots of counts. All. All of the counts."

L: "Yeah. So, so and that's very...You don't... I think you can't...You can't do those things without a sense of responsibility and - and anxiety. Because what is your role? And I think that's where the cultural hangover comes from, that sense of being told that you cannot enforce your politics. You cannot enforce your opinions. You know, and there's. And where does that line come from?

From between positively promoting something and just showing possibilities and different perspectives and acceptances. That the same thing could be seen in very different ways by different participants in in a good way, you know what being accepting or something or encouraging or something that was a reasonable thing could very easily be seen as interfering, as manipulating. You know.

What I can't answer is how much of that is rooted in Clause 28 where there was a legal document that kind of said you cannot do that, and and how much of that is just rooted in the context of of being an adult - an outside-of-the-family adult - in young people's lives."

I'm 37. I'm still working in schools. A group of LGBTQIA+ students put a Pride flag up to mark this annual moment. Senior

Leader takes it down. When I challenge this decision, the answer is "I don't like anything cluttering the walls'. I spin around slowly, arms extended; posters, bunting, posters-and-bunting up everywhere in this room.

K: "Hello! You are younger than me. So if you don't mind being the complete voice for your generation of all kinds of queerness in a completely, like, essentialist way, then I'd be really interested to hear from you about a sort of impressions like from your school days."

E: "Had a really good time at school, kind of in, I think, in the grand scheme of things. I was out at school, not in a kind of grand gay sort of way, but just in people knew, like people around the school knew. I think my teachers knew and I had a queer friendship group.

In Sixth Form, no comment was made on the fact that I kind of adhered to the boys' dress code. I was never scared of people knowing really at school... I think it was, kind of, I could see other people around me who were queer...Yeah, it was never a massive deal. Or at least it didn't feel like that or I didn't notice it being."

K: "Do you have the sense that you were being usefully addressed within the lesson content, in terms of sexual health and relationships, things like that?"

E: "No, I don't. I don't think so. I think we had like one lesson on Queerness. But it was more about LGBT rights across the globe, and it was kind of more of a look at these places where being gay is illegal, and look at the punishments that you might get in that place... nothing about like like what safe sex would look like in kind of non-heterosexual relationships.

Uh. The extent of the canon of queer relationships being addressed in that settings was kind of like that they exist. Umm. You know, in the basic kind of way, like a man could be with a man, or a woman could be with a woman. These are things that exist and we shouldn't be mean to people for doing that, but it was kind of never really... um.. on any kind of like deeper level, like in sense of what a straight person might learn about. the relationships they might have in future. That sort of insight."

I'm 38. I'm walking down a corridor at work, off to explain another red flag on my search engine. This whole HR procedure seems designed to shame. LGBTQIA+ students who are not out at home have been using my work computer with my permission for specific purposes. One has searched the term 'am I a lesbian'. One has searched the term 'gay rape help'. One has searched for 'free trans binders'.

I'm glad it is me being called in to explain my 'highly inappropriate search history' and not them. They've got enough to deal with and are being supported in ways that don't involve being called to meetings like this one. The search terms 'am I straight?', 'free binders' and 'rape help' produce no red flags. LGBTQIA+ colleagues are closeted at work here and intend to remain so. I'm very much not closeted and am no advert for being out at work. Even our IT algorithms think there is no place for queers in school.

E: "I think now that I have more freedom like financially and like expressive freedom to kind of like get the clothes that I want and can like invest in pieces make me feel happy and express my....

So, I cut my hair and got gay little tattoos and piercings and stuff and I think there is like a part of me that kind of wants to go back to my old school looking unquestionably Queer. To be kind of like a visible presence... because I think still some people think that like you can't necessarily have...I mean, I I just remember it always being really kind of exciting or kind of like a big deal whenever like if we saw someone in the school who...

I remember there being someone who was there for an interview. And as I sat around with my friends, we were a few meters from them, but they had like a coloured shirt on and an undercut, I think, and I remember being like 'Guys, there's someone [like us] here'. I have thoughts about [going back] more and more and yeah, I think I do want to be visible when I go back."

K: "I'm wondering if is there an emotional piece to that for you about being in the school that you went to, presenting as the person you know that you are, in this space where I guess some of that was emerging in some really tentative and tender ways. Whether there's something about that for you that would be psychologically interesting or useful?"

E: "Yeah, I think, I think part of it is like I was not very confident.in school. I think, I mean like a lot of my friends have - so friends from home that I don't see very often- have said I'm way more confident now and and I am and I think part of it is kind of I want to go back and be all like 'look, I'm who I'm meant to be now. I'm kind of happy with myself now. This is me now. Thanks for your help along the way'. Yeah."

K: "I'm reminded of sitting next to you on your sofa and reading your personal statement for university. You hadn't sent it, you were drafting it at the time, and I remember asking you 'do you feel uncomfortable with being read as LGBTQIA+?', 'do you feel uncomfortable with being a leader?' I don't know if you remember that conversation, do you?"

E: "I remember having mixed emotions about my personal statement, like wanting....I think it was like 'it is an important part of who I am and how I see things and an important part of my life, and historical interest' But also kind of being quite like, 'oh, this makes it quite official if I...'"

K: "Was there a bit of that classic like, 'oh no, what if it is a massive homophobe in the Admissions Office reading this?'"

E: "I think I had enough faith in the system that there would be kind of checks in place [against homophobic discrimination]."

K: "Woah."

E: "I don't think I knew necessarily about or understood in any comprehensible way about kind of like non-binary identities until like age 16. And by then I had like interacted with people who were [non-binary] but I didn't really get it and I feel like I know it would improve people's experiences of school a whole lot if the number of people who have like a basic understanding of these identities kind of went out from being like a handful of people to... you know, ok, most people just haven't got like even a basic knowledge. Opposition - a lot of that is based on the unknown or like not understanding. Let's say that I would like to fix everything because kids can be mean, because they want to be mean and that's what happens like a lot of the time, but I feel like if people were informed more, it would be better."

K: "Some people, I think, genuinely define trans identities as... they align with the idea of trans people as very threatening, which is... I think I said this to you before, but like when I was doing lots of campaigning for equal marriage, I remember flyering people in the street in London at one point and people saying to me, you know, 'if if the gays can marry, then it undermines my marriage', you know, and they genuinely believed that.

And I do wonder sometimes even now, do they still feel that? I've got the kind of montage of faces in my head. And I I like accept that that was their genuine belief that their marriage would be undermined if gay couples could get married. And I just think, I wonder if their marriages have survived, like, are they still married? Like, how? Errrm. What are the day-to-day effects of gay people getting married on their heterosexual marriages of of many years standing? And I kind of imagine that they are ok, or I would hope that and I would hope that they they weren't negatively affected despite their intense fears. And I think, like I do wonder sometimes about like trans stuff.

Whether, where the fears would be realised. I don't... I'd like to hope not again, but it is hard to be an object of fear, again. And. Errm. How schools navigate that, I think is... Do you think like greater guidance to schools would be useful?"

E: "Greater guidance would not be useful."

K: "I guess it depends on who is making the guidance, right"

E: "I feel like at the moment, greater guidance would probably come down to making things a lot more difficult for people to, yeah, provide support. I feel like any legislation that would be put into place now would be harmful if it came from kind of like a national level. Umm.

I do worry that something similar to Section 28.might happen....I do think, how different my life would have been if [Section 28] was still in place or if it'd been like taken away earlier. I think it would have been different if I if I was being in secondary school, five years, 10 years earlier than I was, yeah, even if it still wouldn't. If it still wasn't in place. The kind of leftover culture that could have been... umm."

K: "Yeah, I mean, I've definitely worked in schools where really it was still in place, although it's not on the books anymore. Like it was definitely... certain schools operated, yeah, almost entirely.as if it were still A Thing. I did wonder about that being like a force of habit, yes. But also, in part I had to recognise that it was because it sometimes it echoed the actual beliefs of decision makers in school. And that was quite, that's quite errmm let's go with 'interesting' to face. Yeah, there's a lot to hold, isn't there? How do you think your life would have been different if you had been educated under this legislation?"

E: "I think a lot of the reason that I realised that I wasn't straight when I did was because I had a lot of kind of openly Queer people around me. And I think it would have been a lot unhappier... I think I would have tried to kind of like edit myself more to kind of like fit in...If I'd have had to kind of be dealing with those worries or or having to keep like this secret and not being kind of like quite relaxed and easy in it, I I don't think I would have done as well at school. Because I was very happy being at school."

I am 39.

K: "Where are we at?"

L: "It's different. It is different now. I think that, you know, we have an LGBTQIA+. community, you have a space to meet. We have Pride events. So, there is a more kind of sense of inclusion and positivity and promotion. I think the tension now has moved to gender, transgender issues. That's where schools are tying themselves up.in knots... I would almost go as far as describing it as a wilful ignorance around that. There is like an unwillingness to engage. And I think the same anxiety in schools around dealing with it - in relation to how a parent is going to react to this - exists, as used to exist around sexuality."

K: "I have felt like a massive increase in difficulty in schools and life since the Gender Recognition Act consultation, and of a kind that feels super, super familiar."

L: "It's like we're 20 years ago, 20 years ago, yeah. And like, people. People who I mix with, I socialise with friends who would never dream of making homophobic remarks? Cannot get their heads around... And then I've got one friend who's a massive... who knew?"

K: "Ohh, I'm really sorry. Yeah, I've got some too."

L: "Oh."

I am 40.

L: "How did this happen?"

K: "And so the last like, biggish piece of activism I was involved in was around the UK Policing Bill. Specifically around safeguarding the right to protest and what that did was it put me in contact and, ermm, purposeful collaboration with people who really wanted to protest against my human rights very genuinely.

And it's been quite mind-blowing to think about, like, how do we all fit together and about common purpose and like how that can be found. And also as I'm speaking, I'm reminded of when the Gender Recognition Act consultation results came out...a group of trans women who I have got very loose connections with. And the first thing they did in like the actual first reaction, in terms of what they did after that horrific reveal, was that they started to they they went, 'ok, so this just happened. So we know that reproductive rights are next.

So what can we do to campaign and safeguard reproductive rights in the UK?' And I thought, 'gosh, that's very generous. I'm just here swearing, I'm feeling bitter and these trans women who will have literally no personal recourse towards these services are already organising and trying to protect reproductive rights in the UK'. Because we're from marginalised positions we can see like the thread of what happens from the like historical or wider perspective sometimes, alternative view, or or... I don't suppose there were a huge many sections of society who heard that GRA consultation result and thought, 'ok, reproductive rights are next.'

Do you know what I mean? And so it's like, how do we understand or remind ourselves how we link together? And also like, what a huge act of generosity. They blow me away. They are such amazing women and and, you know, like they're right and knew it and not many people wanted to listen or understand like what the connection could be. So you sort of think, 'well, how do we...how do we bring our different threads and understand that we're a fabric?' That's quite an interesting question for me at the moment. Yeah. I don't have an answer."

L: "No, I don't have an answer. And I think I I think the the kind of the sadness and the weakness in society is that there still exists that desire not to look for those threads and actually it's 'there's my group' and, you know, another group is competition. You know what I mean is competition or or is likely to hinder the success of our cause because they're, you know, they're jumping on the bandwagon and that's gonna muddy the water. There's a lot of that that goes on, still isn't there?"

K: "I think what I learned from this whole UK Policing Bill actions thing is like a lot of people are scared. Everyone cares about their friends and family. Most people want to make the world better, often for their children, but people's concepts of who 'their children' might be is very varied, and does that make sense? And people's understanding of what 'better' is and what or who it is that symbolises what scares them is also very varied."

L: "It's absurd and I think that's absolutely right. Absolutely right. Because you know. Umm. Yeah, no, it is. It is. And I think, I think I can kind of, you know, I see myself in that to a certain extent. You have a, you have a kind of sense of the - I don't know, maybe that's getting older or or, but maybe I've always been like that- a sense of kind of like your spheres of influence. And and I've never really felt like I kind of have a sphere of influence in the political sphere. But I feel like I can make a difference on an individual level.

Does that make sense? I have a sphere of influence... young people... And that can be powerful and profound and is an important responsibility to kind of think about, but but I I've never really engaged in changing the world in any active political way. It's just not, you know.. you and I, we've lived very different lives in that perspective. I can see E getting involved in that. And then that would be me like about how my how I, you know, manage my anxieties around that. And and feeling proud and scared in equal measure and how that all goes on, you know. Umm."

K: "I want to reflect back to you, you know, a kind of socially inclusive revolution, I think it takes lots of different people doing a lot of different things. And I think as somebody who has worked in schools but also as somebody who loves you, like, I don't want you to underestimate the impact that you have had on me and I'm sure other people in terms of like empowerment and critical thinking and like, just love and what that can do, you know, I mean, so I think that does change the world. So... thank you."

I am 41. And I'm here, telling you all this.

CHAPTER 11

I Don't Remember Section 28

BY CARRIE MARSHALL
(SHE/HER)

Carrie Marshall is a writer, broadcaster, musician and parent from Glasgow. She sings in the anthemic rock band HAVR and her memoir, *Carrie Kills A Man*, was published by 404 Ink in November 2022.

Content Warnings
Homophobia, Transphobia

PREFACE

I narrowly escaped Section 28, but the climate that led to it caused decades of damage. During my school years the press, in cahoots with religious extremists and bored millionaires, demonised and defamed LGBTQIA+ people of every kind, abusing their power to punch down on the powerless and tell us to hate and hide who we are. And now they're making a sequel.

I DON'T REMEMBER SECTION 28

I don't remember Section 28. It was checking in just as I was checking out: just weeks after it was introduced, I said my permanent goodbye to the school I hated. As an apparently cis, apparently straight sixteen year old boy who was barely attending school before finally quitting it completely, Section 28 shouldn't have affected me.

But it did, because I wasn't cis, I wasn't straight and Section 28 didn't plunge us into darkness overnight. The darkness was already there. Section 28 just made it official.

I don't remember Section 28 because I didn't think I was LGBTQIA+. I knew I wasn't like the other boys, and I knew that I was doing a really bad job of trying to be one. But my school's embarrassed, embarrassing sex classes barely discussed reproduction, let alone anything else, so I had to get my knowledge from elsewhere. TV, newspapers and my mum's magazines filled the void. And from what they taught me, I couldn't possibly be LGBTQIA+. I didn't fancy boys, so I clearly wasn't gay, and while I didn't feel like a boy I definitely didn't want to have surgery to have sex with boys, so I couldn't be a transsexual either. Unaware that there were more colours in the rainbow than gay man and straight tran, I reached the obvious conclusion: there was something terribly, shamefully wrong with me. But LGBTQIA+? Me? I couldn't be.

My schoolmates disagreed. When Section 28 was passed, I'd already endured three years of a homophobic and transphobic bullying campaign that would continue long into my twenties. People didn't really distinguish between homophobia and transphobia back then; the shouted slur "poof" was the preferred expression of both, and I got to hear it a lot. There were other slurs, but "poof" was the one that other boys preferred to shout from cars, across streets or in late-night calls to the family landline.

The bullying made me cancel my university plans, convinced that continuing education would continue the campaign. And it made me too fearful to ask girls out, because if they discovered my secret, and I was certain the bullies would make sure they did, then they, their parents and their peers would run me out of town with pitchforks and flaming torches.

There's a joke I like: at school I was bullied for being gay and a girl. It turns out they were right.

Of all my lessons, that one took the longest to learn.

I don't remember Section 28, and I don't remember knowing any gay people, bi people, trans people or ace people. In my teenage world they simply didn't exist. They were only sighted in sitcoms, variety shows and the occasional dad-bewildering *Top of the Pops*. As far as I could see, LGBTQIA+ people lived in my television, not in my town.

We cannot be what we cannot see, and in my teenage years I could not see that there were other people just like me. Section 28 and its cheerleaders wanted to keep young people ignorant and our elders in fear; the information I now pick up so casually in high street bookshops or order from Amazon was not in my local library, let alone my school one. In a world made of rainbows, we were only allowed to see black and white.

I know now that LGBTQIA+ people were keeping their heads down. Social attitudes surveys from the time show anti-LGBTQIA+ sentiment at record levels, with some 75% believing that same-sex relationships were wrong; the chance of a teacher at my school coming out and keeping their windows unsmashed or a gay couple walking down the road arm in arm without violent objection was pretty much zero. Of course, I know now that I went to school with gay people, with ace people, with trans people. I just didn't know that at the time, let alone understand that I was one of them. That took nearly thirty more years.

I don't remember Section 28, but I remember the stories that helped create it. Section 28 had many parents, but the ones vilified by my parents' newspapers were called Eric and Martin.

Susanne Bösche's book, *Jenny Lives With Eric and Martin*, was an innocuous photo story about a five-year-old girl who lives with her dad and his boyfriend and who regularly sees her mum, who lives nearby. It was written to help battle prejudice, but in the UK it became a target for it. Its depiction of an ordinary family doing ordinary family things was recast in tabloid imaginations as "homosexual propaganda", with The Sun's front page headline "Vile Book in School: Pupils See Pictures of Gay Lovers" above an article claiming – falsely – that the book was available in school libraries. It's important to note here that the book was not age-inappropriate in any way, let alone obscene. But it dared to show gay people existing, and as far as the tabloids and Tories were concerned, that made it a menace to society and a useful weapon in their culture war.

The newspaper campaign against Bösche's book was a key milestone on the road to Section 28, with the right-wing press printing ever more ridiculous lies about LGBTQIA+ people and their allies.

Their exaggerations, distortions and fabrications painted the Labour Party and progressives as dangerous extremists who, for reasons and via methods never adequately explained, would turn your children gay and give your hard-earned tax money to one-legged Black lesbian single mothers on heroin. The invective, rarely corrected, was cynically effective. Outraged readers kept buying newspapers and kept voting Tory.

I don't remember Section 28, but I remember the campaign against its abolition. For months around the millennium, Scotland's streets were decorated with dog-whistling "Keep The Clause" billboards courtesy of an evangelical millionaire's astroturfed "grassroots" campaign, a campaign that was almost entirely virtual and played out in pasted-up posters and in the pages of newspapers. Our national press screamed about imagined gay sex lessons in Scottish schools and claimed that Section 28 was the only thing stopping our innocent young children from falling into the hands of predatory queers. They didn't use those exact words, of course. They didn't need to. They rarely do.

A millionaire, the editor of our national tabloid and Glasgow's Roman Catholic cardinal formed an unholy alliance and waged a very public war against LGBTQIA+ people for month after vicious month. As the assistant secretary of the Scottish TUC, Rozanne Foyer, told *The Guardian* in early 2000: "Keep The Clause spent huge sums of money on inciting homophobia, spreading misinformation and stirring up false concerns and fears among Scotland's parents".

They even held their own unofficial referendum. Most Scots rightly ignored it – of the nearly 4 million ballots sent out, only 1.26

million valid votes were cast – but some 1,094,440 people still voted against the abolition of Section 28. That's a quarter of the entire adult population.

Many of those people are still here.

I don't remember Section 28, but I know what it did. It stigmatised, demonised and demeaned LGBTQIA+ people; it told queer kids to be ashamed of who they are; and it forced queer adults to stay in the closet for fear of the most terrible consequences. It banned the books in which we might have seen ourselves and been encouraged to imagine brighter futures, and it enshrined in law that LGBTQIA+ people were second-class citizens. Under the guise of protecting children it damaged a generation of them.

Today we hear from the survivors, but I wonder how many kids didn't survive at all.

I don't remember Section 28, but then I don't need to: they're making a sequel. This time it's ostensibly just for trans people, but of course they won't just stop with us.

Section 28 was largely a creation of the right-wing press, and many of the people, publications and proprietors who contributed to the anti-gay panic back then are at the forefront of the anti-trans panic today. Piers Morgan used to mock gay people in The Sun; now he mocks trans people in the Daily Mail. Andrew Neil published AIDS denial at the Sunday Times; now, his Spectator magazine denies the evidence for trans healthcare and hate crimes while the Sunday Times claims that children are being "sacrificed" to the "trans lobby".

As a teenager, I saw the Prime Minister claim that children were being "cheated" because they were being told that they had "an inalienable right to be gay", in a conference speech designed to delight the Telegraph, the Sunday Times, the Sun and the Daily Mail; now, I get to see the candidates for the job of Tory PM currying favour with the same papers by punching down on trans people.

This isn't history repeating, however. This time it's not just the right wing. The bigots have allies among the very people who you'd expect to be on the side of the angels: the BBC, the Guardian and The Observer, among too many others. Some of the very people who were targeted by tabloids in the Section 28 era now peddle the same scaremongering about trans people that was once aimed at them, their heads turned by lovebombing on social media from people who used to wish them dead. Most pathetically of all, there are even handfuls of pick-me trans people who'll happily throw the entire community under the bigots' bus in the hope that they'll be the last ones to be run over.

It's all so horribly, sickeningly, wretchedly familiar. Once again we are told we need to "protect children" from a sinister "lobby", an evil "ideology". And once again that poisonous narrative is peddling hatred towards the entire LGBTQIA+ community. Just look at how supposed "reasonable concerns" about trans kids' healthcare have become death threats to Drag Queen Story Hours, at the widespread use of "groomer" against LGBTQIA+ people and allies online, at the growing number of reported anti-LGBTQIA+ hate crimes. What's printed in tabloids and broadsheets is amplified on the streets. And as US Republicans are currently demonstrating in states such as Alabama and Arizona, Tennessee and Texas, worse is coming.

Abolishing Section 28 didn't abolish homophobia, transphobia or any other -phobia. It just told the people who had those views, that quarter of the population that voted to keep the clause, to be quiet about it. And now those people are being given permission to be loud all over again.

CHAPTER 12

The Shadows

BY JOHN NAPLES-CAMPBELL
(HE/HIM)

John is an award-winning teacher who has worked with the Scottish government to make the curriculum inclusive. A passionate activist, he strives to make schools a safer place for the LGBTQIA+ community.

Content Warnings
Homophobia, Transphobia, Violence, Bullying

PREFACE

On 21 June 2000 (with a 99 to 17 majority vote with two abstentions) history was made in Scotland when Scotland repealed Section 28 via the Ethical Standards in Public Life (Scotland) Act 2000, one of the first pieces of legislation enacted by the new Scottish Parliament. LGBTQIA+ Education was now lawful in Scottish schools after years of legislation stating that schools "shall not intentionally promote homosexuality or publish material with the intention of promoting homosexuality."

Twenty-three years have passed, and the shadows of those days still echo in our school corridors to this day. They were beginning to fade, slowly, but in recent years voices against LGBTQIA+ education and support for transgender students are beginning to raise their heads again.

As an openly gay teacher and the first in Scotland to be given recognition for my work in LGBTQIA+ Education by the General Teaching Council for Scotland, I have been at the forefront of how LGBTQIA+ has progressed through the years – the good, the bad and the just.

In 2018 we reached a historic milestone when the Time for Inclusive Education campaign (which I lead the secondary education section on) was successful when The Scottish Government announced its intention to introduce LGBTQIA+ inclusive education in all public schools with cross party support. After eighteen years... LGBTQIA+ people will finally have a voice in classrooms without it being a postcode lottery of the passion or enthusiasm of the teacher leading it.

So let's have a look at the diary of a gay teacher in Scotland...

2000

An undergraduate teacher starts university, wanting to change the world – eager to learn and make a difference! He has started his journey and his classroom will be one of acceptance, the repeal has happened, but no training has been given to staff on how to deal with LGBTQIA+ Issues . What can we discuss? What can we say? Are we allowed to talk about it now?

The ban on lesbians and gay men serving in the United Kingdom armed forces has been lifted. Jack and Ethan are dating on *Dawson's Creek*, Willow and Tara kiss on *Buffy the Vampire Slayer* and by the end of the year the age of consent across the United Kingdom is about to be equalised to 16 from 18. Young people are watching gay people on TV and are talking about it to their friends in the playground, but PSE classes still don't talk same-sex relationships and gay teachers are still in the closet.

LGBTQIA+ Groups are non-existent in schools across the country and posters from Stonewall, LGBTQIA+ Youth Scotland and TIE are nowhere to be seen. There's an urge to move forward but the steps are delicate, and it's still whispers and trepidation.

2005

He's now an openly gay teacher in his first school but he is having classroom management issues with a difficult S3 class. He is newly qualified, trying to be authentic, and wanting to succeed. He's asked for help but instead of giving educational advice his head teacher reflects on him being openly gay, assuming that this is the issue. He leaves feeling dejected and questioning why he feels like he's back in High School under Section 28. Is this what his career will be like from now on?

2010

He's been working in this school for 3 years and is loving it. It's forward-thinking and the staff and students are a community. The Equality Act has come into play and things are slowly beginning to move, finally, Equality Act posters are seen in schools which show the overview of the act for all to see, which reads that LGBTQIA+ people are now a protected characteristic.

Stonewall posters of 'Some People are Gay – Get over it' are beginning to line the school corridors and a small rural school in the East coast of Scotland enters a film contest with Panasonic with a short documentary called 'It Gets Better', sending a message to all students from the group of S3 students that their school community is one of acceptance and equality and surprisingly to the group... wins the UK prize for Global Citizenship. The award-winning group of young people create a LGBTQIA+ school group open to all and speak at a Stonewall Conference about their work.

2015

New school and new council. He now works in one of the biggest schools in the West Coast. He's asked by the Head Teacher to use his knowledge of LGBTQIA+ Education to create a training for staff – mandatory for all teaching staff. He delivers Equality training and how to feel confident in delivering LGBTQIA+ inclusive education as well as tackling homophobic and difficult language or opinions. We are starting to see teachers wanting to do more, Stonewall are offering training for staff to move forward with embracing LGBTQIA+ education in their schools, LGBTQIA+ Youth Scotland have launched their Schools Charter programme and posters for inclusion are now in classrooms and school corridors across the country.

Faith schools are still facing some backlash but the Equality Act is helping things to move along a little. He wears a 'GAY' t-shirt to an LGBTQIA+ Assembly and a fellow member of staff comes out to all students, students from the school's LGBTQIA+ community speak openly about their own coming-out stories, and a fire in ignited within the student body. They want more. An LGBTQIA+ group is created, a safe space is found in the school and they start a new journey where they are at the forefront of the councils plan on equality and diversity. It feels good! It feels promising!

2020

He's been on a journey. He's been rejected for numerous leadership posts and he's questioned if his work in gay rights in schools has had something to do with it. Is he too progressive, even years after the repeal of Section 28? He will never know, but that is the legacy of Section 28... the feeling of not being good enough for a society. He's now getting married and finds himself in another part of Scotland, in another council and another school. Things aren't as progressive as they should be, but they are getting there.

The council and the Head Teacher know change is needed and are embracing how to make it successful. It feels good although social media, for all its good, it has had its flaws too. He has found, along with others wanting inclusive education that he has been branded a 'pervert', 'paedophile' and even had death threats.

For decades, the LGBTQIA+ community has been subject to homophobic propaganda which paints us as a threat to children by claiming that we are paedophiles, child abusers, groomers. Until recently, we believed we had moved on from those dark days. Sadly this is not the case online. He's happy with what he's achieved and knows that teachers across the country who are authentically their gay-selves or who are allies are supporting school groups and making huge differences to our young people and their futures.

The Time for Inclusive Education campaign has succeeded in their aims when the Scottish Government announced that it had accepted the recommendations of the Working Group in full and would be embedding LGBTQIA+ themes across the national curriculum by March 2021. LGBTQIA+ groups are now common in most schools across the country, staff are being confident in approaching the Senior Leadership Team about how they can do things better and faith schools are looking at how they can embrace a more inclusive education. Difficult conversations were had along the way, debates and words connected to Section 28 days were still often heard, and frustration meant that at times we felt like giving up, but passion drove us forward.

2021

It's the end of the pandemic and he's been appointed as a senior leader in a small rural school in the Highlands of Scotland. To say goodbye, and continue on their progressive journey, they hold a PRIDE day – full of love, laughter and rainbow flags. A pride party picnic is held in the sports field and he leaves for the summer with a smile, knowing that equality has taken a huge step and that students feel safe and secure in their learning environment.

After summer he steps foot into his new school; confident that he's finally been appointed as an openly gay teacher as a senior leader - only to find out that a complaint has been raised with his appointment and his support for transgender young people. He has to have an awkward conversation with his new Head Teacher about his sexuality, inside he's screaming and crying – it feels like school all over again. The rejection, the fear and the anger. This is not the start to his career in this school he wanted. He tries to move on but is challenged by staff on 'why' they need to have an inclusive education supporting LGBTQIA+ young people.

The triggers are starting to manifest onto his physical and mental health. He's hounded on social media by scores of people supporting anti-trans ideology, and referred to as a 'groomer' and 'paedophile'. As a victim of childhood sexual abuse, he's broken by these comments.

2022

International Women's Day (and also his birthday) he receives a handwritten, anonymous card to the school. It reads 'Fuck off out of our school you big poofter. Our kids don't ned a shirt lifter around them'. He's left in utter shock as the school day is taken up with police interviews. It's not a student, it's come from an adult, and he tries to figure out how to move forward. A hate crime has been recorded to the police. He feels like he's walking on eggshells. He tries to do his job but doesn't know who to trust and who to turn to.

He begins to be micro-managed by his Head Teacher, gaslighting him that it's not the 'community'. Two months later another card arrives, it's the same handwriting. He hands the card to the Head Teacher and bursts out crying. This one reads 'Still here? Time to Go – shirt lifter. Repulsive Man'. Police now log it as a hate crime and stalking also discusses with him the tone of it being a threat. The trauma and triggers are too much. He's taken back to the bullying of high school, the feeling of not being good enough, not being accepted.

He leaves the school that day knowing he won't be returning. He's signed off work and is diagnosed with Post-Traumatic Stress Disorder. His council are supportive and he finds a line manager who listens and acknowledges his experience but he feels his career is over.

2023

His confidence in his ability and his profession has gone. The experience has had a negative impact on his marriage and his personal life but everything is being 'talked through' and things are looking better. He has been surrounded by love and supported to continue the important work of creating safe spaces for all; no matter their gender, sexuality, religion, race or disability. He sets foot on the yellow brick road once again.

The journey is real and the legacy of the Local Government Act, Section 28, is buried deep in many who went through it. Being gay was something to be ashamed of. Today, it isn't, but it still isn't easy. A recent report found that 59% of young people had witnessed an increase in prejudice-based posts, comments, and/or attitudes online whereas 48% of young people have faced transphobic comments online during lockdown.

As a teacher we have a duty of care over young people to educate them. No-one stepped in to help me back then and I feel a bit angry about that to this day. It's amazing when you speak to young people about moments we have gone through and they can't believe that things were so different not that long ago. Words such as 'agenda' and 'promoting' are still heard from those who do not fully understand the notion of inclusive education.

We have moved away from LGBTQIA+ education being about sex education and it's now about looking at those who have contributed greatly to our country and curriculum areas, it's about 'normalising' family structures and seeing ourselves as the LGBTQIA+ community the classrooms we teach and learn in. Some staff still feel reserved about approaching the topic through backlash, some schools are still targeted for being inclusive and doing forward thinking, and some students feel they can no longer carry on being bullied for being who they are.

It's important that we remember that when we repealed Section 28 a massive vacuum was left. We are slowly filling this – It's a reminder that every young person deserves to learn in a safe and secure learning environment, that is the true measure of the attainment gap. Health and Wellbeing is the responsibility for all.

CHAPTER 13

Smalltown Boy

BY KESTRAL GAIAN
(SHE/THEY)

Kestral is an author, playwright, poet, and voice actor known for activism and speaking out on LGBTQIA+ issues. She is the author of *Hidden Lives* and *Counterweights* among other works.

Content Warnings
Bullying, Violence, Homophobia, Conversion Therapy

PREFACE

The following stories happen in chronological order, and depict my life over a ten- year period. Starting in 1993, this is a look at my life leading up to the repeal of Section 28 in England, Wales, and Northern Ireland.

Naturally in a book about Section 28 I have focused on the impact that the law had on my life, my queer identity, and some of the difficulties I faced growing up. There were, of course, happy days, birthday parties, smiles, love, and laughter during this time too - but it's impossible for any memoir to look back and capture a complete picture of every contextual factor of every day of someone's life.

During the time period these stories cover, I thought of myself as a cisgender gay male, and my use of language throughout the pieces respect my identity at the time rather than my identity now. At the time of writing I consider myself a feminine non-binary person who uses both she and they pronouns.

Thank you to everyone who gave me love and support during the time that this story covers. To my parents, friends, and all the other incredible people that helped me get through school and showed me the kind of unconditional love that I didn't have for myself - I will never be able to express how profoundly positive an impact you all had on my life.

We must fight to ensure no more young people go through these kind of experiences - that nobody grows up feeling the kind of shame, erasure, and hatred that Section 28 promoted.

FIRST LOVE, FIRST SHAME

I started secondary school in 1996, but I knew that I was queer far before that. The first time I used the word 'gay' to describe myself was when I was eight years old, some three-and-a-half years before I got to 'big school' where it would start to be used as an insult.

My small-town primary school was based in an old Victorian school-house with a couple of wooden mobile classrooms tacked on to the side. The bottom halves of the walls were brown polished brick; the upper halves were painted with a thick light-green paint that would flake off in large patches. The lights hung from tall ceilings on long, thin wires, their glass globe lampshades swaying ominously whenever a breeze blew through the building. The class-rooms were littered with old wooden desks and chairs it hurt to sit in for too long, and the closest thing we had to modernity was the giant TV and VCR that would occasionally get wheeled between classrooms for us to watch the odd documentary.

I'm not sure where I first heard the word "gay", but I both knew what it was and seemingly knew that I was it. My parents, liberal as they were, didn't really have any openly gay friends from which I'd have heard it, so I can only imagine it was from a newspaper headline or TV show that I had seen my older brother watching. This was early 1993, and it would be years before questioning queer children would be able to gingerly type the words "am I gay" into their inter-net search engine of choice. Being romantically attracted to other boys was just a fact of life for me, a truth I had always known, but at some point that truth grew a label, and that label was "gay".

I had a number of teachers at that school, but the one I remember most was Mrs B. She was warm, encouraging, and she was one of the first people to tell me that it was okay to find things hard sometimes. She wore glasses with octagonal frames, had a bob of gingery hair, and I'd often observe her biting her nails at her desk when she thought nobody was watching.

She was my teacher twice during primary school. The first time was in 1992-93, the same year I'd come to refer to myself in my head as "gay". My first kiss happened that year, too. I had a small number of other boys I considered friends at primary school, and one lunch time we were playing hide and seek and two of us found ourselves hiding under the coats in the cloakroom. There I was, pressed up against my friend, hidden from view, and I remember turning to him and whispering "hey, wanna be gay together?"

Seconds later the two of us were engaged in a snog that would only stop when the sound of the cloakroom door brought us back to reality. At eight years old we knew what being gay meant - but more importantly we knew that it was something to be hidden, to be kept secret. I would kiss my friend a lot in the coming few years until he moved away, but never once did we even acknowledge each other in public after that day. He was my first love, and also my first shame.

The second time I had Mrs B as a teacher was in my last year of primary school, year six, in 1995-96. The school had got hold of a couple of computers from the Computers for Schools scheme, and one of them sat gloriously in our classroom. Mrs B, knowing my love for anything digital and electronic, would often hold time on the computer over my head as a reward for finishing my maths work - the one subject at school I found intrinsically hard to grasp.

I remember my last day of primary school really clearly. There were assemblies and awards, of which I won none, but then we had free time in classes in the afternoon to just chill with our teachers. Through the lens of modernity I think Mrs B would certainly have been described as an LGBTQIA+ ally, but in the 1990s it was enough that she implicitly made space for the weird and different kids in her classes. That last afternoon was no different.

With our last hour of the day she got us all to sit in a big circle where we got to talk about what she dramatically referred to as 'the future'. At eleven years old I'm not entirely sure I had a well-formed concept of time and age, but I certainly knew that the transition from primary school to secondary school would be seismic. She'd go around the table and ask people what they wanted to do with their lives, and a few people talked about what they had to do because they were good at maths, or because their parents wanted them to do a certain thing. Mrs B seemed annoyed and asked us all why she didn't like it when people said that.

I raised my hand and said "because we can be anything we want to be?"

"Yes!" she exclaimed, jumping up from her chair and giving me a momentary hug before returning to her seat and enthusiastically telling the class "you are the only ones who get to decide who you are, and you can be anything that you want to be. Good. Yes." As I gathered up my things to leave the tired and dated classroom where I had spent much of the past year of my life, she turned to me and said "Best of luck. I'm proud of you."

Years later, after a chance encounter in a supermarket, we swapped addresses and exchanged a few letters. I asked her if she had known that I was queer, and she said she absolutely did. She spoke of the times she wished she could educate her classes, and tell the queer kids she taught that her classes were a safe place to be. That there was nothing wrong with them, and that they were valid and beautiful and valued. But she was honest about why she never got to say those words at the time. "Had I ever dared to speak out, even in the staff room, I'd have lost my job."

CONVERSION CONVERSATION

The move from primary school to secondary school felt more like being transferred from a place of learning to a high-security prison. Several times the size of my small-town primary school, young people from all the other small towns and villages in the area would bus into the behemoth collection of ageing buildings every day, swarming down corridors and pathways in groups and cliques like a plague of social anxiety made flesh.

I started at that school in September 1996, and remember my first year there through dark, dystopian lenses. The cold metal-framed windows, the lockers covered in graffiti, old wooden desks, orange plastic chairs, and those rolling chalk boards that kicked up the dust of a thousand half-taught lessons with every squeaky move. The wave of school modernisation that a New Labour government would introduce was still a few years away, and every single building we traipsed in and out of for lessons seemed to creak and groan with disdain.

My year 7 form tutor was a short man called Mr J who looked like Elvis Costello and talked like Derek Trotter. He said that we could always come to him if we had any personal problems, but I remember one day, after him calling someone he didn't like 'queer', thinking that he was the last person on the planet I'd want to talk to about who I was and how I was feeling.

With my be-gay-with-me friend having moved away, and the sudden influx of words like "gay" and "queer" being used as an insult, I was back to feeling completely alone - like I truly was the only gay in town. Words like "bender" and "bummer" were often used to describe people that were seen as weird or different, and most of our teachers smirked or encouraged this language rather than dissuading it.

I learned to keep myself to myself. The less I did to draw attention to myself, the less I'd be noticed. Or so I thought. I used to sit in the corner of the form room and read books or do homework - earning me the status of 'geek' or 'weirdo' or 'nerd'. Somehow a rumour started that I was posh, in spite of the fact that I came from a not-that-well-off family. People started to pay attention to me, and I spent more and more time hiding in either the IT room or the music department.

I struck up a friendship with a girl in my form called S that had a speech impediment, which drew the same bullies that I had and made it easy for us to hang out and try to avoid them together. She and I would spend time together at the start and end of every day comparing notes on our favourite bands and talking about music and clothes. Gossip would have you believe that she and I were dating, but the two of us had an unspoken understanding that, really, neither of us were the other's type. It would be another two years before we had the courage to come out to each other. We both knew, but also both understood that it was something to be hidden and treated with secrecy and shame.

At the end of my first year of secondary school, my parents separated and my dad moved into the spare room of Anthony, one of his friends from work. Over the next twelve months Anthony would go on to abuse me - but it would be a number of years before I actually saw it as abuse. At the time, he framed it as a relationship and I was over the moon with all the attention and time that he gave me. I thought I was in love with the much older man, and as previous experience had taught me that anything even remotely homosexual was to be strictly kept a secret, our affair became another secret that I kept from the world - something to enjoy on the weekends I visited my father.

The 'relationship' came to an end when my dad moved in the summer of 1998, almost a year after he'd moved in. Distraught at the idea that I might never see him again, I wrote Anthony a love letter and gave it to my dad to pass on to him along with a gift that I had delicately wrapped in cloth and string. My dad called me later that evening to tell me that Anthony had read the letter and that "a number of beers were drunk and a number of tears were shed." In retrospect my father must have known what was in the letter, and known about our relationship, but must have decided for whatever reason that it was best to ignore it and move on. To this day we've never once discussed it further.

That September, just a month after the relationship came to an end, I started my third year of secondary school. Heartbroken and feeling more alone than I ever had before, I began to develop anxiety and depression. My friend S noticed that something was wrong and I told her all about Anthony and the breakup... but I omitted the fact that he was in his late 20s and a friend of my dad. She told me to stop being so dramatic. "No boy is worth crying over," she'd often say to me. Perhaps not, I thought, but this man was.

I was convinced that nobody would ever love me as much as Anthony had. He often told me that he was my saviour, he was the only person who saw good in me, and that without him I was nothing. Lonely and heartbroken, I started overeating and occasionally throwing things back up afterwards. My skinny frame became a little more rounded, my personal hygiene became poorer, and eventually a teacher noticed that I didn't seem to be doing well. I got referred to the school counsellor.

Mrs P wasn't really a counsellor. I'd later learn that no laws or policies existed around who could call themselves a counsellor, and Mrs P was a friend of the headteacher who came into school one day a week and talked to the 'weird' kids. We'd sit in a cupboard in the humanities block that had a couple of ageing comfy chairs and a stained old rug, and she'd ask me all sorts of pointed and uncomfortable questions about my personal life.

I decided to confide in her about many things - but not that I was gay, nor that I had recently been in a relationship with a man in his late 20s. I knew that those things were still off limits, things that people didn't talk about. What I did decide to tell her, however, was that I'd had a bit of a strange relationship with food the past few months - and that I was occasionally eating so much that I'd vomit afterwards.

With a horrified look on her face, she rushed out and got Mr G, the same teacher who had told me to go and see the school counsellor in the first place. He immediately called my mother and told her everything I'd just said to the school counsellor. I remember being mortified as I sat at home with my mum later that evening, her asking me why I was doing these things and what I hoped to achieve. I just said "I don't know" over and over, but I think she knew that it was a lie. It was a lie - I knew exactly why I was hurting and the effect it was having on me. I also knew I wasn't allowed to tell anyone.

I was assigned six subsequent sessions with this counsellor, during which she repeatedly asked me if I was gay. I would always say no, but she would spend almost every session telling me how hard life would be if I 'decided' to be gay. She told me of AIDS, of a life without love, and described in detail the evil people in history who practised homosexuality.

She never used religious language or framed things as a 'sin' to God, but she certainly made it clear that homosexuality was something to be cured and conquered, not celebrated or embraced. I kept my mouth shut, and failed to turn up to the final two sessions. The school didn't check back in with me, and I always made a point of taking the long route through the humanities block so that I never had to walk back past the cupboard-turned-counselling-room again.

THE MILLENNIUM BUG

I started studying for my GCSEs in September 1999, and while the world was preparing for the momentous turn of the millennium I was busy preparing myself to deny all the rumours that were spreading across the school about my sexual orientation. My being gay was somehow an accepted fact, in spite of the fact that I had never confirmed or even hinted at it. Even when I started actively denying it, people still thought I was 'that gay kid' as if it were a fact we had to learn for our upcoming exams.

My friend S didn't like the attention I was getting and, desperate to remain in the closet, decided to stop hanging out with me for a while. She had always been fierce in her resistance to shaving her arms or plucking her thick bushy eyebrows, but one morning that term she came into school with thin brows, makeup, and a new haircut. She started dating a boy in the year above, and we stopped talking on the phone or discussing music. I guess we all had our ways of coping.

For the turn of the millennium my mum drove us down to Devon to stay in a bed-and-breakfast owned by one of her friends. A few other people my age were also in attendance and, determined to appear normal, I proceeded to engage in a heavy make-out session with a girl my age.

The next day, we all hung out again - only this time the girl I'd been kissing had to look after her little brother too. At one point the conversation turned to kissing, and he excitedly exclaimed to the group "I really want to kiss my friend Steven at school". Others in the group laughed and told him that he wasn't allowed to say things like that, and he'd learn that it isn't okay to want to hug and kiss other boys. I joined in, telling him that boys didn't like other boys. My ears grew hot and I felt intense shame rise within me. Perhaps, I thought, the real millennium bug was something far more sinister than a computer crash.

In January 2000 I met V, a new student who joined my year group after transferring from another school. She and I were instantly drawn to each other, throwing my sexuality into confusion. We'd talk video games and poetry, and excitedly exchange news about the upcoming SEGA Dreamcast console. We tried to date a couple of times, but I couldn't quite reconcile my feelings of attraction with my certainty that I was gay.

We remained good friends and, many years later, he would come out as a transgender man and we'd laugh about what we didn't know when we were teenagers. Section 28 didn't just mean we had no representation - young trans people like us were forced into cis-heteronormative boxes because we lacked the language, and any kind of visible role models, to know any different.

In June 2001, after our final GCSE exam, everyone in my year group bought notebooks and got our friends to sign them. I handed mine around to everyone, even though I'd only really ever had two friends in my time at school. When I got the notebook back, pages and pages were filled with slurs like "seeya bender" or "glad I'm getting away from the shirt lifters." There were, however, a number of pages at the back that seemed to have a little more in them.

S, who I hadn't been close with since her transformation in 1999, wrote me a small essay covering more than three pages. She spoke of her shame, of how she wished she was stronger. She finished with the words "sorry for being such a shit person", and I read it with tears in my eyes and a pain in my heart. I wanted to tell her that I loved her and forgave her, but couldn't quite find the words. I hope that, deep down, she knew.

The only other person to write anything other than a slur in my end-of-school notebook was V. Beautiful phrases like "we will always have love for each other" in impeccable handwriting filled almost two pages. I knew that I had hurt V at times, but also that this was a friend I was lucky to have.

I thumbed through the rest of the 50-page notebook and noticed several drawings of dicks, lots of "wish you was dead" and "gay bender faggot" scrawled in different handwriting using a variety of pens. In between the bigotry were the occasional "good luck for the future" message from a teacher or member of staff, who clearly saw the slurs and chose one last time to turn a blind eye and pretend that they weren't there.

CHICKEN BURGER CALAMITY

The summer of 2001 felt strangely liberating. For the first time in a long time I had no schoolwork to do over the summer, and at sixteen I was old enough to get a job on the checkouts at the local Safeway. Being exposed to more people, and being able to spend more time on the internet getting to know other LGBTQIA+ people, I grew in confidence and started to feel a little more pride in who I was. September 2001 rolled around, and I looked forward to starting my A-levels with a nervous degree of excitement and trepidation.

My school wasn't big enough to have its own sixth-form, so it teamed up with three other local schools and called itself a 'consortium'. What this meant in real terms is that the handful of students from each of these four local schools became one big cohort, and got bussed between the various schools for lessons to ease the timetable and resource burdens of running further education post-16.

In September 2001, at the start of Year 12, my year group simultaneously shrank and grew as a result. Most of the worst-offending bullies and homophobes didn't stay on, instead taking on apprenticeships and jobs. Buoyed by my newfound confidence and a lack of haters on every corner, I began to stop denying the rumours surrounding my sexuality. I remember one day in our sixth form common room confirming for the first time that yes, I was indeed gay. "Are you actually though?" people would say to me, followed up with "we always called you it, but like, as an insult. We didn't know you actually were."

At the very start of that school year we went on a residential to London so that students from the four different schools could bond. For small-town kids like us, London was the epitome of style and the capital of culture, and we couldn't wait to spend a few days exploring the capital. There were various different activities for us to sign up to, and I excitedly combined my love of music and nerd life by signing up for both the trip to see Les Miserables and the afternoon at the SEGA Arcade in the Trocadero.

I still didn't have many friends from my own school, and realised as the escalator to SEGA World ascended inside the Trocadero that I knew nobody else who'd decided to take part in this activity. Once we were inside the arcade, a trio of boys from one of the other schools ushered me over. They didn't know me, nor had they heard any of the rumours about my sexuality, but they correctly surmised that I was a fellow nerd and wanted to hear my opinions on which SEGA console was the best.

The boys introduced themselves to me. One of the trio, whose name I learned was B, wanted someone to play Dance Dance Revolution with - and as a fan of flailing my legs around like some sort of camp *Riverdance* performer, I readily agreed. He beat me mercilessly several times, and we went on to play several other games together, all of which I was terrible at. The day, and residential, grew to a close. On the coach home we all swapped MSN Messenger details - the cutting edge of technology in 2001 - and went our back to our respective hometowns to prepare for the start of actual lessons the week after.

That weekend, B popped up online while I happened to be signed in to MSN Messenger.

"Hey"

"Oh, hi"

"How're you doing?"

"Good thanks, still tired from London!"

"Yeah me too, it was so fun though. Thanks for hanging out at the SEGA arcade!"

"It's cool, I had a really good time."

The conversation continued until, shaking like a Polaroid and acting on a complete whim, I typed the following:

"Hey, can I tell you something? I'm gay."

There was a pause.

"Promise you won't tell anyone? I'm gay too. I've never told anyone that before. I'm shaking like a leaf."

We started dating a few weeks later, and the relationship lasted just over eighteen months. We even decided to go to the same university, although we broke up before we quite got there. In time he and I both came out to more people - including our parents.

I told my mother that I was gay - and that B was my boyfriend - on the morning of my 17th birthday. She didn't act surprised, confirming my suspicion that she already knew, and told me that it was fine and normal. She did, however, unintentionally add to my own internal homophobia.

As a teenager who had finally, after years of repression and secrecy, been able to be honest about who he was, I was naturally excited to live my truth as vocally as I possibly could. I distinctly remember a time when my mum had guests over, and someone made a joke about us all being in a *Carry On* film. I responded with something like "well at least I can be Kenneth Williams!" and my mum replied "while it's very nice that you're in a relationship with a boy, you don't have to keep bringing it up every five minutes."

I was mortified, humiliated, and it's something that I play back in my head to this day. Words are powerful - and with no positive role models in the media and no education or acknowledgement of LGBTQIA+ lives at school, hearing my mother tell me to keep my sexuality more to myself just reinforced all the feelings of guilt and shame that the years had taught me to feel about myself and my identity.

B was still in the closet, and wanted to keep our relationship secret. That was fine with me, but everyone in my year now knew that I was gay and it only took a couple of awkward questions about whether I had a boyfriend for rumours to start to grow. While I successfully managed to deflect attention from B, the fact that I was not only gay but had an actual real-life boyfriend took about three days to spread through the entire school.

People from other year groups started coming up to me in the corridor to ask me if what they had heard was true, and I became somewhat of a fascination to the waves of bigots and homophobes who suddenly realised that calling me "gay bender" had become more of an affirmation of truth than an insult. I noticed that teachers actively avoided me more in the halls, and many refused to talk to me at all.

Miss H was our head of sixth form, and a suit-wearing hairy-armed woodwork teacher. She was an archetypal lesbian stereotype, and took pity on me after rumours of my sexuality hit the staff room. I'd sit in her classroom sometimes at lunch when the bad-mouthing from other students got a bit too much, and she'd play me Tracy Chapman and talk about queer culture. I adored her. While she'd never confirm it, I knew that she was queer like me and an ally should I ever need one. Seeing that someone like me could go on to not only thrive, but work with young people - something the press seemed so against - gave me immense hope for the future.

One day I got called in to see Mr G - now promoted to deputy headteacher. I stood in his office while he sat at his desk and looked at me sternly. "Is it true that you and B have been holding hands in the common room?" he asked me.

"Yes," I replied.

"Do you think that's okay?"

"Well, lots of couples hold hands and kiss in the common room, sir."

"Oh, so you're a couple, are you?"

"Yes."

"Well stop it. It's not appropriate, and if anyone sees you do it again we'll have to ban you from the common room. You have to keep things appropriate while you're in this school."

I left his office, and B and I never spent time together whilst on school property again. Once a week or so we'd walk into town to a local bakery and buy pastries for lunch, sit on a bench in the local park, and talk about all the amazing things we wanted to do in the future. The rest of the time we just hung out with different people during the school day, which meant I'd often go and buy my lunch from the school cafeteria and go sit in Miss H's classroom to eat it alone.

One such lunchtime I was stood queuing for a chicken burger. In the days before Jamie Oliver's healthy food campaign, a good school lunch always consisted of a chicken burger with cheese and mayo and I stood there, burger in hand, waiting to pay so that I could go eat in peace. I thought I saw the queue move and, in a world of my own, stepped forward and accidentally walked into the boy in front of me, a tall ginger-haired kid from a few years below.

"Oi, what do you think you're doing?" he said.

"Oh, sorry, my bad," I replied.

"Oh, you're that gay kid. Do you fancy me or something?"

"No. Believe it or not, I don't."

"Ewwwww, you fancy me, don't you?"

"No, I don't fancy you."

The next thing I knew, there was a fist flying towards my face. I remember pain, I remember being on the floor, and I remember tasting metal. I got up, noticed blood on my hand and shirt and, in shock, got back into the queue and paid for my chicken burger. Not a single member of staff intervened, and everyone stood in relative silence as I gave the dinner lady my pound coin and shuffled off towards my tutor room.

My form tutor, Miss B, was young and trendy and liked *Buffy The Vampire Slayer*. She looked horrified at what I can only imagine was a somewhat bloody seventeen-year-old, and asked me to explain what had happened whilst handing me a tissue. On explaining the situation, she immediately went to seek support from another teacher.

I was hoping that Miss B would go and get Miss H - but instead, Mr. G walked in. The same Mr G that, weeks prior, had told me off for holding my boyfriend's hand in the common room. The same Mr G that forced me to see the school counsellor a few years prior. He wanted to know why I had just started a fight. I reiterated my story, and waited for what I hoped would be a reasonable solution and perhaps some medical attention.

Mr G signed and shook his head. "See," he said, "this is exactly why I told you to stop being so inappropriate. It's not fair on anyone, and now you're starting fights because of it."

I tried to question what he was saying, but he moved on quickly to what he called "reasonable next steps". I was to be suspended for a week, he decreed, for starting a fight in the school canteen in front of "several witnesses". The boy who punched me would receive no further punishment, and I was not to try to talk to him, go near him, or "try to recruit him" again. Dazed, bloody, and sore, I left the school and went home to bed.

I spent the week of my suspension avoiding my mum, which was relatively easy given how much extra work she seemed to be doing at the time. All I had to do was disappear for a bit in the morning so she thought I'd gone to school, and she was always home long after school would have finished. I didn't tell her about the fight, or that I was spending my days at home that week. I even intercepted the letter that got sent home about it. I just wanted it to go away.

So instead of seeking help or support from my family or friends, I hid my face until it had more or less healed, wept into my pillow at night, and wondered if the rest of life was going to be like this too.

This was the era of Section 28.

CHAPTER 14

Queer Things in the Shadows of the Lamplight

BY GEORGE PARKER
(THEY/THEM)

George Parker is a writer and performer. They were crowned Disabled and Queer Artist of the Year in 2022, and they are the co-founder of Empowered Talent. They host A. G. Parker's Cabinet of Curiosities podcast, and co-host Rebel Riot Poetry.

Content Warnings
Death, Homophobia, Transphobia, Violence

AND THEN MY HEART OPENED LIKE PETALS

I want to die like a magnolia tree blossoms:
open, relinquishing all I have in a final blaze of beauty.
I want to die like a magnolia tree:
bloomed luxurious, dark earth beneath my feet,
my roots stretching into what is rich and fertile,
my heart scooped out
and set upon a breeze.

I do not wish to die encased in shame.
I do not wish to die condemned
by the same government I helped to win a war.
I do not want to die beaten in the streets, I do not want to die,
outcast alone,
because of who I am, who I love, for
whatever way I do not fit
within the margins drawn up and etched in stone
not even that long ago.

And I do not want to die with the bits of twisted wire
that were used over the years by vicious gardeners
to bend me into a shape that was not mine, yet
still etched upon my body.

I want to die like a magnolia tree,
having thrown all my colours into blossoming skies –
nothing hidden, nothing held back
in full bloom.

I want to die like a magnolia tree blossoms:
open, relinquishing all I have in a final joyous blaze of beauty.

TWO STORY TOWN

Two gunmen, chins and barrels raised, face
each other in a red dust part of town.
The next street over,
and a moment later
the dust is redder,
someone will say,
Two shots
fired simultaneously!

But
the gunmen know:
one squeezed the trigger first
and had to watch
as the other,
leaking red,
pulled theirs too late
and
from the barrel
no bullet fired; instead,
there flicked
a ribbon tongue
that said,
I love you.

ALL OUR PRIDE

How beautiful it is to see our city lit
with ecstasy – rich with joyful glittering pride,
faces shining, heads held high, vibrant colours far and wide.
Perhaps, I hope, it's all our pride.

And hope I find, bridges unintended lies, draws lines to where we
hope we'll be from where we actually stand today.
'Cause yes, this rainbow splendour wends its way
transforming streets of concrete grey,
embracing most with wondrous flow,
and yet, I fear, some feel alone; the step to here
a steep plateau and not a welcome pathway home.

Because prejudice not yet outgrown means some of us
remain unknown, have become invisible,
been rendered mythical entities
by the media's portrayal of our own identities,
and the extremity of these illusions prevents
our everyday inclusion – makes it a forgone conclusion that we must
hide, trapped inside a warped disguise that
I invite you: take the time, cast aside, see what you find.

'Cause if you don't, It's All Our Pride remains
a beautiful but hollow line, that time after time
many marginalised queers have seen
is a lie. 'Cause we've been made other,
our various colours of the rainbow still treated

like sideshows, and thrown too easily away
or under the bus.

Even amongst queer clubs, we know,
this social plateau will leave us alone, our
hopes and dreams littering the pathway home.

But amongst the fool's gold glittering I think
I see a glimmering of real hope and Power, too,
so long as you remember: the first pride was a riot
inspired by violence against queer lives,
defying those who think we shouldn't thrive,
shouldn't rise, and while we fight to survive,
they play us off against each other, try to make us forget you're my
Muslim brother, my trans sister, my black, brown, Asian, Christian,
pre-transition,
gender glistening, queerness bristling comrade.

Pride is how we rise above those who would deride us,
make healing circles from the lines
they tried to separate us into of opposing forces,
because they know our voices forced apart
might not be loud enough to banish lies that tell us
we aren't enough, we aren't welcome, we aren't perfect exactly the
way we are.
And together, we aren't minorities.

We're marginalised,
fed lies to divide us create tribes within tribes,
but Pride is hope cut and dried,
mixed with pain and glitter, ground
into gunpowder, raising our voices louder,

hearts fired up and fist-ready,
ready to connect because when you hurt one of us, all
of this proud crowd will circle around and
protect and nurture and heal,
fists in the air, shouting our truth. Holding our ground.

Pride is helping those who would drown
without us, 'cause the first pride was a riot led
by a black trans woman, Rest in Power.
Now, if you feel you might cower
remember our founders, the gender confounders,
the courageously boundless, system devourers
hear their shouted chorus now saying,
Don't ever bow your crown to the ground!
Be proud. We follow in the footsteps of giants, so
Holler loud!

Pride is fuck your rainbow dollar
and every capitalistic notion that
keeps us pinned down, reduced to body, reduced to cyn-
ical money-making, booty-shaking, don't-the-straights-love-this-
particular-rendition-of-queer?
Reduced to the value of labour, this wage-sum worth, this tiresome,
zero-sum game that
leaves us feeling like dirt,
always looking for something to fill the gap,
the hurt they wedged between our hearts,
focused on parts of ourselves and the ones we can't have, the ones
they'd deny us,
use to drive us out of our minds, drive a gap between
this brand and that brand of human, makes us ask,
Are you the thin edge, fat edge, better-off-dead edge

of a wedge we didn't even agree to pick a side of,
and which is merely a slice of the so-called
ultimate prize dangled before us, and is incomparable
to the wealth those in power wield to keep us wanting.

Pride is us all here, today, knowing
we can only be who we are
and that that is enough.
Look around you, you are encircled by love.
You are loved. You are love.

Pride is self-love and acceptance that we fire
in each other, love that if we all truly nurtured its truth, those
preaching against us would quake in their boots.
Imagine: our hellfire heartache raked together,
set ablaze, its rolling mist of brimstone haze would
break the daze, help others escape the cis-het maze,
would shake the tectonic plates of structural
oppression harder and more profoundly than any
earth-shattering orgasm any
individual could get while high on gender euphoria,
but get high on gender euphoria.

Strap on a dick, flick a bean, be seen, be queer,
be the fullest expression of love that only you can be.
'Cause conveniently there's no-one listening
as we scream for justice in the name of one another,
when we say, This is my family.

Our peculiar alchemy a blasphemy to all crushed
by the gravity of the unjust majesty of patriarchy, of callously constructed systems of oppression

that try to stop us from remembering:
the first pride was a riot incited by violence
against queer lives, defying those who think we shouldn't thrive,
shouldn't rise, but they just inspired us to help each other survive.
Black, white, disabled, dyke, Asian, Trans, femme, fags, cripples,
butches, lezzers, Bis, homos, aces, it's
All Our Pride.

We're marginalised, fed lies to divide us make
tribes within tribes but Pride is to reside in Love,
abide in Power, never to cower but to think of our confounding
fathers, to remember we're members of our proud family, this happily queerful rebellious army, free
not to beg to be included, but to instead create a
new reality as together we fight for trans rights,
accessible nights, for us all getting to bask in ecstatic light and hold
our heads up high because

Pride is a goddamn riot
and together,
we can change the world.

GYNANDROMORPH

In 2011, a great Mormon butterfly,
wings like David Bowie's eyes,
emerged under a chaotic sky, a surprise to all as it fluttered,
flaunting different magpied colours on either wing.

Like
someone had taken a pen and drawn a line
down the middle of this queen/king.
Like gender was a thing it had maybe had a fling with once
but didn't fancy calling back.

Gynandromorph.

Each half its own unique wonder:
one half thunder the other a summer field of buttercups.
It's like they couldn't decide what to wear,
who to be upon coming out so, they did it all,
their cocoon a small portal to immortality,
or at least the feeling of it anyway,
because that's what gender euphoria feels like –
when you get it right, you know:
you have the power of a god within your bones,
you feel at home,
owned by no one but yourself,
ready to create outward from your point of truth,
knowing you'll fight tooth and nail
for others who are like you and different from you

and are utterly themselves.

Gynandromorph;
it's when a creature is born
div i ded,
half female, half male. It's both, it's neither.
It happens in a range of species, including spiders and birds,
is unheard of in humans and
there's a range of theories about how it occurs –
mostly about sperm – But, maybe
it's also a wish.

People laud this bug for turning into a butterfly,
create bumper stickers, fridge magnets,
sing its praises under the guise of well-wishing saying,
'It turned into something beautiful, you will too!' Forgetting
this butterfly had to totally dissolve into goo
before it could re-emerge as something admirable. Well,
when it feels unpalatable
to live in your skin, you've got no choice but to begin again,
to go beyond what's imaginable and into the unfathomable,
and that takes considerable strength. But I bet
you'd go to any lengths to do it again.

Because I don't know if anyone told you this but
you can't be anyone you want to be
you can only be you and who you're meant to be.
and I am queer of gender and sexuality,
and I can't and wouldn't want to change that any more than I could
my disability.
Queer is how I am not bound
by the rigid structures of society, of how we should be.

Queer is vulnerability and the finest armour,
folded and hammered, folded and hammered into something
unfuckwithable. Not caring if it's socially permissible.
Queer is the ebb of gravity as I slip into the streams of possibilities
that are held within nature's palms and within that word 'queer'.
Queer is freedom; queer is beauty unabashed. It's
strong thighs like the stem of a flower
holding beauty up, open to the world.

Queer is how I don't fit and it's how I am at home.
Queer is every soldier of that cishetpatriarchy mown down,
scythed like corn and left sweet, delicious for our militia to eat.
Queer is how I embrace the start of each day,
arms wide and open, welcoming the sky and its chaos
and whatever the day may bring because I am of the earth
and I know chaos too.

Queer is knowing that I am the chaos of the sky
and just like that butterfly, I can't hide.
I can only be me. But I see how lucky I am that
I can do that.

Now it's 2021 and I've dissolved a hundred times,
wrapped in trauma like a cocoon,
and each time I've considered emerging
I've thought, What this outfit?
No, I want both. I want neither.

I want something bespoke, created just for me,
not one of those rigid assigned-at-birth labels
that comes with a list of expectations and restrictions.

I want to re-emerge as something undeniably me
that says to the world,
you're free to invent yourself.

GROWING UP IN SUBURBIA

When I was young, I was so
macho
hoping machismo would keep me
safe, turn bravado to brave, that
eventually I'd start showing up, not just
saving face. It
took me a while to realise days
had drifted by and I
still hadn't landed a single one,
feeling like I was the only one that didn't fit –
no dick and tits not big enough to
satisfy society's expectations. So I
disengaged. Found new ways to punish
my body, flog the feminine out
of me, chastise the curves for not being curvy enough and my
heart for not being hard enough because hardness
and armour were to be looked at with
admiration.

They said, Open up, but what they meant was
Hand me the means by which I can
pry your ribcage open,
analyse the raw insides, place
shards of your intimacy on the scales and find them
wanting. I am
wanting. I want. I

want another go. This time,
I promise myself, I'll show.

STEPPING OFF THE GENDER WAGON

Call me blessed, for sweet anonymity
free to live with the golden impunity that comes
from being read as straight, cis, able.

Only that's not reality. That's just a fable...
Sooner or later, I'll use a stick, share a kiss. Forget to fit.
As a kid, the village in which I lived
had the feel of a brass band march –
conservative, claustrophobic and starched –
steeped in the patriarchal drone
that orchestrates our children at school and at home,
tells them to grow up, to go line up
into two neat rows: sweet pink girls, brave blue boys.
It pins us with its perpetual noise.

Its rules might not be obvious, but all are insidious.
Groups, neighbourhoods, clubs swell and form
the same as in the animal kingdom: comply and conform
and you're in; threaten the status quo and you're out. So...
Non-binary is a boundary I draw to keep the patriarchy out.

Dr Fausto-Sterling
talks about cultural myths of differences found
between those of the opposite sex
'Without complete social equality we cannot know what they are.'
Well, that equality thing seems a bit far from
reach right now... and biological essentialism is right here.

These structures find ways to influence you, the way you behave:
Rewards for being passive, for treating men as a saviour,
punishments for being 'rowdy', 'unladylike', 'wayward'.

And for men, oh, they have to be manly as hell and want only
to conquer a fifties bombshell.

When maybe they'd just like to wear her dress...
But gender isn't gender expression and it isn't sex.
This warped conflation has created a mess.
And this is what goes on inside of my head:
It's bullshit that some personality traits and jobs are deemed masculine.
If I prefer those, then what then?
Were my female role models not strong enough?
Should I have persisted and gone through life trying to bluff
my way as the woman I don't feel I am?
Did I idolise my father, devalue my mum?
Does it mean I'm not a feminist? Does this make me sexist?

We live, unless lucky, in a lab rat's maze –
shamed for stepping outside society's ways,
and rewarded for succumbing to it.
It's made my gender feel like something unwieldy,
like a sword too heavy, brittle, unyielding.

And I think it best, until the world figures out, we're not
pink and blue – that there's a rainbow of other colours too,
that I just put it down. Step off the gender wagon. So:
Non-binary is a boundary I draw to keep the patriarchy out.
but damn that drone is obnoxiously loud. It's continued too long,
forcing all of us who don't have a permissible song,

to nonetheless open our mouths and legs and from there, too,
have that drone come blaring out.

Well, I am too strange for everyday rhythms.
It's weird to be stranded in someone else's kitchen
with the girls. Who decided genitals were a good way to divvy us up?
I don't put much faith in this gender construct.
Thank the universe then for ear defenders!
And two fingers up to there being two genders.

Alok Vaid-Menon becomes a lover's thighs wrapped around my ears,
Telling me its ok to not live life in fear –
the songs of other queerdos drowning out that
gender, gender, gendered expectation –
a perfect, joyous non-binary vacation.
No more will I sit legs crossed, beating that drum;
Why pick a gender? Must I be only one?

No more will I sit on a dining hall floor
reciting the hymns of men who think
they have to clip our wings, that gender is something set in stone.
Fuck that! I've even begun composing my own.
Note by boundless note I am playing myself into existence.
There's a reason I left brass band land behind.

The world deserves me unhindered, no gender in mind,
not giving a fuck about expectations.

I can't leave my potential latent.

I'll continue to flout the societal norms that lead me to doubt
my own unique song that that drone has shouted over for so long,

well, from the gender wagon, I dismount.

Non-binary is a boundary I draw to keep the patriarchy out.

CHAPTER 15

Just a Phase

BY COLIN MACKAY
(HE/HIM)

Colin Mackay is a late bloomer, having eventually accepted he was gay and coming out at 35. He is part of the UK software community, and is currently helping set up an LGBTQIA+ network at his workplace.

Content Warnings
Homophobia

A lack of suitable Sex/Social education classes led to a stunted understanding of what loving relationships can look like.

I was 13 when Section 28, or Section 2a as it was in Scotland, came into force. At the time I was blissfully unaware of the impact it was having on me. Despite Scotland managing to rid itself of this heavy-handed legislation three years before England, the damage had been done. It took me a further 10 years once the legislation was rescinded to untangle enough of the damage to even accept that I was gay.

In my high school, our social or sex education (SE) classes were taken by a teacher who'd agreed to the extra workload along with their regular classes. I understand they got some sort of additional compensation for this. For my class, we got a rather ineffectual French language teacher who had enough problems containing his class during French lessons, let alone the titillating subject of relationships, procreation, and parenthood.

As a result, SE classes were a rowdy affair and I don't think much was gained by them, even by the straight cohort in my class.

Relationship structures, as discussed in the class, were very much the formal variety. You meet, you "court", you propose, you marry, you have children, they grow up, and the cycle repeats. It was almost like a production line from the perspective of a product making its way through the factory.

Somewhere along the way, someone did ask a question about gay relationships. The class went wild at the question with lots of innuendo being thrown about. The teacher did nothing to answer the question, of course. He did his best to calm the class down, but it just wasn't his forté. Somewhere in the verbal mêlée I think someone did try to be "helpful" and suggest that it's usually just a phase.

Somehow that stuck with me. It's just a phase. It wasn't an expert voice. Just some random pupil in a classroom who had as much understanding as anyone else in the room, which was close to none.

That was the sum total of gay relationship education I got at school: "Just a phase".

So, when I got a bit of a crush on the French exchange student I was assigned, I told myself to not think about it. It's just a phase.

When I got a crush on Wesley Crusher on *Star Trek: The Next Generation*, it's just a phase.

As this went on, I started telling myself that I wasn't really getting crushes on men, I just happened to be good at telling what an attractive man looks like and appreciating that beauty, like appreciating the beauty in a painting.

With all this constant self-talk about how it was just a phase that I would grow out of, I started trying to get involved in more "straight" activities. By this time, I'd left school and was at university. I know... looking back with hindsight this would have been an excellent opportunity to get involved in their LGBTQIA+ societies, but I never did.

In my first year, I joined the Christian Union. (To those that know me now, yes, really!) I didn't find God, or Jesus, or anything really.

All the other people saying they felt Jesus's love and I felt nothing. One person there had an air of serenely knowing his place in the universe and I just didn't seem to get any clarity at all. No epiphany about when these feelings would end. It's still just a phase, why isn't this helping?

In my second year, a friend in my class was talking about going to football games with his brothers and I expressed an interest in joining them. They supported Dunfermline Athletic, a small club that still had terraces as it wasn't in a high enough league to require a fully seated stadium. So, I started going to see football matches. Real men watch football. Straight men watch football. This should help, right?

However, it was such a homophobic environment that all it did was push my real feelings further down. Each homophobic jibe, regardless of where it was aimed, was used to push down and repress my real feelings because by this time, I shouldn't have them. It was just a phase, after all, and it must be coming to an end soon.

Friends and colleagues had made jibes about my inability to notice attractive women. One time walking back from a sandwich shop to the office, the two very straight colleagues I was with had their eyes out on stocks watching an attractive woman walk up the street - meanwhile, I was monologuing about the serendipity of trying a new filling in the baked potato I'd bought for lunch because they didn't have the filling I wanted. After that, every time there was an attractive woman in the vicinity, they'd make a jibe about how I was more interested in coronation chicken than women.

I was getting more concerned about this phase I was in, as it was getting on for 10 years since that singular piece of gay relationship "advice" because the school couldn't teach about different relationships, except for the government-approved man plus woman relationship escalator to marriage, all for to make babies.

Then in my mid-twenties I got into a relationship with a woman. Finally, I'm normal. It was just a phase after all!

However, I wasn't happy. The relationship didn't last, and 3 years later I was single again.

In the years that followed, I tried to unpack what had happened. There was a lot of homophobia pushing down on my real feelings, so I was feeling pretty disgusted with myself every time I thought about attractive men.

However, two things happened that helped a lot.

The first was an unfortunate side-effect of the previous relationship I was in. My girlfriend was toxic, and she'd managed to alienate my friends. So, now that I had none, I had to make new ones, and it turns out not having friends making low-level homophobic comments really helps.

The other thing that happened was when I was sent down to London for work, and I got invited to a pub quiz by a friend. He said that he'd invited some other folks that I'd probably get on well with. That's the evening I met Seb. He was the first unapologetically gay person I'd met. He was very open about himself and didn't hide, or understate anything euphemistically. He was friends with all these straight people who didn't verbally bash him for his sexuality.

This was an education. A real education. Not in the boring rote-learning mechanical disassociated classroom sense. It got me thinking about myself and how I'd been cheating myself because I'd been repeating this once-heard mantra that it was "just a phase".

It turned out that Seb and I had similar jobs and would meet at conferences and the like from time-to-time. Each time, I noticed how most folks didn't treat him any differently, they liked his company, and even although they were straight, they didn't make derogatory remarks about his sexuality. It gave me confidence to examine myself and my own feelings. I eventually began to accept that I was gay myself.

Then at one conference in Manchester we were both at, I asked if I could talk to him in private as I needed his advice. We headed out to the smoking area in the hotel car park, and I came out to him. Technically, he guessed, as I stumbled around a bit trying to get the words out, so my coming out was just me saying "Yup!" when he asked if I was trying to come out. We ended up just talking for about 45 minutes and it felt that a massive weight had been lifted from my shoulders.

I had not only finally accepted at the age of 35 that it wasn't a phase, but I had told someone, and they accepted me. I really am gay.

The next day on the train back to Glasgow I must have looked like a glaikit eejit, I was smiling to myself that much.

I told my parents a couple of weeks later, and then a few close friends. They all accepted me for who I was.

Now imagine if we'd been able to have proper discussions in school when I was a teenager about same-sex relationships. I see younger people today who do get better social/sex education classes in school, and they have much more acceptance of same-sex relationships and gender identities than my generation ever did.

Even if they are taught by ineffectual teachers who can't control a class, they have access to shows like *Heartstopper*, *Love Simon/Victor* and *Sex Education*. My generation didn't even have that. *Queer as Folk* didn't come out until 5 years after graduating from university.

Section 28 and laws like it stifle knowledge. They hinder the emotional growth of LGBTQIA+ kids. They cause trauma in all sorts of insidious ways. Trying to choose being straight is not a real choice. I'm not, millions of others are not. It was never going to work without causing harm. In fact it did harm me and many others.

CHAPTER 16

Sectioned

BY ELY PERCY
(THEY/THEM)

Ely Percy is an award-winning Scottish writer, best known for their novel *Duck Feet*. Their first publication was a letter in *Big!* magazine (1994). Since then, they've released a memoir and two further novels.

Content Warnings
Mental Health, Homophobia, Transphobia, Violence

I was seventeen when I was sent to the adolescent psychiatry unit. It was 1989, the same year the Karen Carpenter biopic came out, and half the folk at my high school were waxing lyrical about slimmer's disease. In reality, none of them had a clue – they all thought eating disorders could only happen to straight cis middle-class girls who looked like supermodels because that's what they saw on telly. Plus, nobody gave a fuck about mental health. Not really. They constantly slagged off the fat French teacher, made jokes about her being half-bulimic.

Hannah Jeffery was the only one who noticed I was slowly shrinking. We weren't even pals by then, having drifted apart during puberty after Hannah discovered the opposite sex; sometimes we'd walk to school together though, and a few weeks into term she began quizzing me about my lunchtime habits and those sandwiches she'd seen me chuck in the bin. I fobbed her off with excuses about soggy tomatoes and how I planned to grab something later from the canteen. Still, she persisted, hovering outside the toilets one afternoon to tell me she thought my weight loss was getting out of hand.

Days later, I fainted at the Wets concert. Hannah, who'd sat in the row behind me and my sister with her own pals, was bawling her eyes out when I came round in the medical tent. I knew I was fucked, but self-preservation kicked in and I went all out in a last-ditch attempt to pass myself off as a fawning Marti Pellow fan: I got overexcited, I said; it was hot, the crowd was claustrophobic, and Hannah – well – she was being melodramatic!

The workshops I'd done at youth theatre that summer helped turn me into a spectacular liar: my mother really did believe I'd got food poisoning three times during the holidays from imaginary dinners I'd eaten at imaginary pals' houses. I'd also taught myself the best tricks for skipping meals and hiding food, the most effective ways of getting rid of things I'd no choice but to swallow.

The young first-aider who was treating me frowned and asked to see the backs of my hands; then she pointed at the bruises on my knuckles and said, "How long have you been purging?"

* * *

The adolescent unit was a glorified jailhouse. There were rules and regulations, weigh-ins and spot-checks; I wasn't allowed sharp objects, couldn't go for a piss unsupervised, and there was a points system called 'parole' where you were encouraged to earn the privilege of going out for incremental walks.

My key worker was a sixty-something Captain Birdseye look-alike who always had bits of food in his beard; he told me seconds into our introduction that he'd no time for attention seekers, and if I didn't eat the meals he brought he'd arrange to have me fed through a tube.

I was given a room of my own with a window in the door, and whenever I closed the curtain to get undressed, Birdshit or some other psycho staff member would barge in and accuse me of trying to hide a bag of puke.

* * *

One of the other inpatients accosted me after my medical that first day; I quickly discovered she was my through-the-wall neighbour, a sixteen-year-old Kate Bush obsessive who'd been diagnosed with manic depression. Her name was also Kate, and she'd the same tousled hair and slightly haunted look as the singer; I liked her straight away, but pretty soon I'd be driven mad by her playing Wuthering Heights on repeat.

Kate asked what I was in for.

"Anorexia."

"That's what Shirley said."

Shirley was the twelve-year-old with OCD who always lugged around a medical dictionary. There were four other inpatients: Julie the Junkie, Pyro Pete, John the Baptist, and Other John.

"So, what's your name, newbie?"

I told her.

"We thought you were a boy!"

"I get that a lot."

Kate smiled at me. "Well, I'm glad you're one of us," she said, "cause now we outnumber them."

I didn't know what to say; I'd never felt like one of the girls.

"You should grow your hair," she added, "you'd look pretty."

* * *

I don't know why Kate's appraisal bothered me so much, but it stuck with me for days. It wasn't like I hadn't been fielding comments about my appearance my entire life.

Both me and my sister had inherited our dad's ginger barnet, but where hers was fine and straight, mine grew outwards like a flaming hedge. My mother was constantly nagging me to make more of an effort, to act more ladylike – she hated seeing my messy mullet paired with oversized shirts and baggy jeans, hated that strangers often referred to me as 'son'. I didn't mind being misgendered – in fact, I quite liked it – but my mother took it as a personal insult and, over time, the feeling that I'd somehow deeply disappointed her began to wear me down. It didn't help that girls at school had suddenly switched from talking about spiral perms and boyband crushes to pubic hair removal and the sex they were having with their actual boyfriends; trying to keep up with those conversations was exhausting – plus, I'd other things to think about, like exams and what was going to happen once I finished school.

I didn't feel so bad about my body image when I was at primary because I wasn't the only one in my class who looked a bit different. Hannah Jeffery had a mushroom haircut and would take her top off on hot days when she roared through the scheme on her BMX. Hannah grew out of it though, grew her hair down past her shoulders, started wearing bras and lipstick by the time we went to the high: she became one of the popular crew who snogged boys behind the pavilion.

* * *

We were still expected to attend school on Mondays through to Thursdays, even though the curriculum in the unit had no relevant academic content. Most mornings, we were herded into a classroom for 'English', which meant watching a film like *Chariots of Fire* then giving your opinion on it, or 'maths', where you'd be folding cardboard prisms. We usually got to choose our subjects in the afternoons: 'art' was making something out of clay, 'tech' was making something out of wood, and 'home ec' was sewing a cushion cover; very occasionally, we had 'social studies' with a retired history and modern studies teacher whose favourite topic of conversation was sightings of the Loch Ness monster.

Classes were supposed to run from ten till noon then two till four, but they rarely went to schedule because things were constant pandemonium. If one of the day patients wasn't climbing the walls, then Julie was shouting about how she shouldn't be locked up with us 'nutters', or John the Baptist was being triggered by something that contradicted his belief system. Pete, who had ADHD, was permitted to do most of his tasks in a separate room, and Kate, who'd been inside twice before, had a knack of scheduling one-to-ones with her psychiatrist to coincide with the dullest sessions; Shirley was usually there in body, but off in a world of her own performing traits of whatever new illness she'd decided she'd contracted, and Other John rarely got out of bed before lunch time.

I turned up for every one of those classes because my mother had put the fear of God into me by saying that if I didn't participate fully then the Family Allowance payments she received for me would stop, and she wouldn't be able to afford to visit, never mind keep me when I got out.

* * *

"Your mum's a bit of a cunt, int she?" said Kate, one night when we were standing against the radiator outside the nurses' station.

"What do you mean?"

I'd become used to Kate blurting things out without context, but this time she'd taken me by surprise. My mother was there every night at the seven pm visiting hour, except on weekends when she came for two hours on the Saturday afternoon with my sister. She always brought me magazines and puzzle books and coins for the pay phone, and she was super friendly to everyone – in fact, other folk's visitors were constantly telling me how amazing they thought she was.

"Well,' said Kate, 'it's twenty past seven and she's been talking to them dicks the entire time."

She meant Birdshit and the other day staff.

I watched as my mother doled out second helpings of homemade fruit loaf from a giant Tupperware dish; baking enough to feed the whole hospital was now part of her daily ritual.

"Well, that's my diet out the window," said Birdshit; he grinned and wagged a finger at her: "You're a bad influence, Mrs Cassidy."

"Also," Kate went on, "sa bit shit bringing cake to the hospital when your kid's in for an eating problem."

I shrugged; "I don't mind."

My mother's ears must have been burning, because I heard her say, "I think her majesty's getting impatient."

Birdshit gave me a royal wave.

"I hope he chokes," I said.

Kate put both hands around her throat and stuck her tongue out; we both sniggered.

My mother's face was tripping her when we were finally alone in my room. "I don't like that Kate McCann," she said, peering out into the hall before drawing the curtain shut.

"Oh, I do."

"Well, I'm telling you, I don't."

My mother had an opinion on all my friends. Most of them were either too cheeky or born liars; and back when they still bothered enough about me to come calling, she would leave them standing on the doorstep. My old pal, Hannah Jeffery, was a rare exception: she was wild, according to my mother, but she'd also once been crowned 'cleverest girl' in our primary class after beating me by half a point during an epic spelling test. This somehow earned her the red carpet treatment at our house, and for years my mother made tablet on a Wednesday because Hannah was coming for her dinner.

My mother started talking about how Birdshit was a lovely man, and how I was lucky to have someone like that looking after me, before launching into a rant about the terrible buses and the horrible weather, and how travelling all this way was a nightmare.

I let her words wash over me, having learnt from past experience that any other response would only prolong her moaning. I didn't bother telling her that her new best pal regularly made crass weight-loss jokes and referred to me as 'Twiggy', or that he'd continued to force me to eat fish fingers after the dietician agreed I could try going vegetarian.

"I'm only going to say this once," my mother lamented. "You'd better be on your best behaviour and doing everything those nurses tell you."

* * *

On Friday mornings there was music and drama therapy. I never got to take part, though, because Birdshit always insisted on having our weekly 'chat' at the same time. This was despite me practically begging him to reschedule. I explained how I loved singing and acting, how the year before I'd played Calamity Jane in our high school show; I even told him I'd been thinking of applying to do a musical theatre degree at the RSAMD in Glasgow, but his response was to roll his eyes and tell me he was far too busy to accommodate my every whim.

I also never got to go on the minibus trips on Friday afternoons. All the other patients went to the cinema or Kelvin Hall to play badminton and table-tennis, whilst I was told I needed to conserve energy.

I wasn't allowed home on weekends either because I was considered at risk and in need of extensive support.

So, Fridays through to Sundays were mostly spent sitting alone in my room, staring out the window.

* * *

Besides school and various types of therapy, we had mandatory twice-a-day 'community meetings'. This was where everyone had to congregate after lunch and dinner to talk about any news or grievances. There was always a delegated 'chair-person' – usually Kate – who read aloud the minutes, and a 'secretary' – usually Shirley – who wrote down whatever was said. Mostly, it was things like a new day patient arrived this morning, or such-and-such has an overnight pass, as well as constant complaints about the meals-on-wheels aka 'the shit truck' and the unanimous objection from the inpatients towards going to bed at nine pm.

I rarely had anything to contribute because I never went anywhere or did anything different; plus, it felt pointless when the meetings were monitored by the day staff who'd made it clear they weren't interested in our opinions.

* * *

The only nurses I didn't hate were the two Elaines who worked the nightshift. They were friendly and funny and more relaxed about enforcing rules like the nine pm curfew; they'd often rent movies and order pizzas for everyone, although they never tried to cajole me into eating takeaway, nor did they humiliate me because I was the odd one out.

It was the Elaines who introduced me to *Prisoner: Cell Block H*. I hadn't watched it before because it was banned in our house because of the 'vulgar' language in it, but I very quickly found myself hooked on the lives of the inmates of Wentworth Detention Centre. I also enjoyed getting one over on Birdshit and my mother, and soon I lived for those Monday nights when we were allowed to stay up after midnight.

* * *

One of my favourite *Prisoner* characters was Judy Bryant, a middle-aged convict who was trying to break out of jail so she could exact her revenge on a 'bent' ex-officer. I don't remember specifically what drew me to Judy – I'd love to say we shared a strong sense of social justice, but more likely I just saw something of my own needs and desires reflected in her, because she later went on to have a plotline where she got out and became a singer.

I didn't realise Judy was queer at first – not till Kate filled me in on the gory backstory about how the officer had murdered her ex-girlfriend. Until then, the only openly gay people I'd seen on TV were either men or Martina Navratilova, so whenever I subsequently watched her on screen I felt this mixture of awkwardness and guilt and excitement.

It wasn't long afterwards that Kate dropped the bombshell about Elaine Parry being gay:

"How d'you know?"

"Heard her telling Elaine White her partner was on that Channel Four thing where the lesbians abseiled into parliament to protest against Maggie Thatcher's clause."

"I hate all that paedo shit," said Julie.

"Men shalt not lie with men," said John the Baptist.

"Did you know that homosexuality's no longer classified as a mental condition?" said Shirley.

"Lesbians are hot," said Pyro Pete.

"I like her," said Other John.

I liked Elaine Parry too. She'd never criticised the way I looked or patronised me with anorexia horror stories; she'd never been anything other than lovely. I also thought she was cool because she wore her hair in a Vanilla Ice flat-top and drove a Harley Davidson.

As far as I was concerned, Margaret Thatcher was an old windbag and consenting adults should be allowed to sleep with whoever they liked. I never voiced those opinions though – didn't want anyone thinking I was that way inclined. I'd heard what a group of 'concerned' parents did to a maths teacher at a school in Glasgow after discovering he lived with another man; it was in all the papers, and my mum and our downstairs neighbour had gone on and on about how he deserved all he got, and how he should *never have been allowed to work with children*.

* * *

As the weeks continued, it soon became obvious that something was going on between the two Johns. They were always giggling and whispering to each other, and they went on parole every day as soon as school was finished without inviting anyone else.

"I think they're gay together," said Kate.

"Better not be," said Julie. "I don't want fucking AIDS."

"How would you get AIDS?" said Shirley.

"Nah," said Pete. "They're just out having a fly smoke."

I said nothing. My window looked out onto the path that led to the bushes where the Johns went for their 'smoke', and I'd seen enough to know that Kate's gaydar was spot-on.

* * *

Eventually I got used to being in the unit, got used to the weigh-ins and the check-ins, and the horrible build-up drinks, and having to keep a diary of everything I ate; I also, to my surprise, began to genuinely enjoy aspects of my time there. This was mostly down to Kate of course, because she was kind to me and she made me laugh, and because she was always hatching hilarious hare-brained schemes to discombobulate the nurses – like the time she sent greetings cards to her least favourite members of staff and signed them "from your bestie, Nurse Ratched".

So when she found out that John the Baptist had been on *Songs of Praise* with his school choir, she insisted on him and me doing a sing-off; and when it became obvious that our singing annoyed certain members of staff, it turned into a whole thing we did every day at four o'clock; and soon all the inpatients were involved: Other John got his dad to bring in his Yamaha keyboard, Shirley abandoned her dictionary in favour of organising the sheet music; even Julie turned out to be a good laugh, and she knew a lot of campfire anthems. It was only when Pete helped himself to a saxophone and several percussion instruments from the music cupboard that the nurses intervened; by then it was too late, because Sally the occupational therapist had heard us and decided we needed more sessions of music and drama therapy.

I started making up my own tunes on the guitar after that, and Kate and I co-wrote the lyrics for a song called *Nut-House Blue*s. I also told Sally about my plans to apply to the RSAMD, and she said she'd do everything she could to help me.

* * *

Then one night my mother brought Hannah Jeffery to visit. It was awkward because I wasn't expecting her, and I hadn't spoken to her since the concert or replied to any of her letters. Plus, I'd just had an argument with Birdshit because he'd tried to make me eat beef olives.

"How are you really?" said Hannah, when my mother disappeared outside to talk to Other John's dad; she had on a men's grey blazer over a white polo neck tucked into light blue jeans, and her hair was now in a platinum blonde pixie cut. I was about to compliment her on the new look when I saw her eye snag on the gravy splatters where I'd thrown my plate against the wall. She didn't say anything, but the horror on her face was clear, and suddenly I felt ashamed and disgusted and deeply, deeply wounded.

"What do you fucking care?" I snarled. "It's your fucking fault I'm in this fucking fucked-up dump."

* * *

Later, I lay in bed thinking about how sad and lonely and angry I was, how I'd taken those feelings out on Hannah who really didn't deserve it; I thought about all the other nasty things I'd said – I'd told her I hated her and never wanted to see her again, that I wouldn't care if she got mowed down by a double-decker bus. Then I thought about all those times growing up when she'd been there for me: how she'd defended me against the tough kids in our scheme, the ones who called me names and wanted to batter me because they thought I was 'posh', because my mother wouldn't let me play football or climb on top of the bin sheds; I also thought about how she'd tried her best to comfort me after my dad died, how I'd pushed her away then as well. But mostly, I thought about the summer holidays six years ago – that wonderful time right before my family went topsy-turvy and our friendship waned – when Hannah and I built a tent in her back garden and stayed out all night playing Top Trumps, and eating Tangy Toms, and pretending I was a boy called 'Allen' so that Hannah could practise her kissing technique.

* * *

Everything changed after Hannah's visit: Julie finally got her wish and was transferred to a drug and alcohol unit, then Pyro Pete became a day-patient and a new girl with the same name as me was given his old room. Kate was discharged despite telling everyone she didn't feel well enough, and Shirley's parents withdrew her from the unit permanently after she nearly died from a burst appendix; Birdshit, who was Shirley's key worker as well as mine, was given his marching orders because he'd failed to do a proper 'wellness check', and because he hadn't bothered to report her complaints of stomach pains to the night staff.

Without Kate and the others, I felt lonelier than ever; and one night, during an episode of *Prisoner* where Judy gets a letter from her homophobic family saying her estranged father is dying, I almost confessed to Elaine Parry that I thought I was gay: I chickened out though, because I was worried it would get back to my psychiatrist, or worse, my mum. Plus, I wasn't a hundred percent sure exactly what I was – I'd always known I'd liked girls, but sometimes I liked boys as well, and a lot of the time I wished I was male. Back then, I didn't know trans people existed, and I was only vaguely aware of bisexuality because of David Bowie; mostly, I just thought I was an ugly fucking weirdo that nobody would ever love.

I wanted to phone Kate and tell her everything – I missed her so much, and I knew she'd never judge me – but she hadn't called or written like she promised, and I was scared she wouldn't want to hear from me now that she was out.

I thought about suicide, but my heart wasn't in it. Then I seriously considered running away: I'd a whole plan worked out that involved a taxi to Buchanan Bus Station, a Megabus to London, and the Johns creating a diversion; I even packed a bag. Then I realised I wouldn't get very far with the thirty-six quid worth of twenty pence pieces I'd saved from not phoning my friends.

* * *

My four-weekly review came around again, and I got a shock when my psychiatrist said he was 'very pleased' with my progress. I was allowed outside for the first time in three months; and this felt like a win, until I started to panic about the weight I'd put on, and whether or not I'd be soon be sent home; because even though I was seriously fed up with the unit, and its suffocating rules and lack of connection to the outside world, a part of me didn't want to leave – because I couldn't bear the thought of going back to school or having to live with my mother again.

* * *

Then the week before Christmas, there was a musical production of *The Picture Of Dorian Gray* at the King's Theatre, and the nurses took me, Pete, Other John, the New Girl and two new day patients to see it; John the Baptist was supposed to go as well, but he'd barricaded himself in his room after Other John announced he was being discharged.

I nearly refused to go too, when my new key worker revealed I was to be confined to a wheelchair for the entire trip. To be honest, it wasn't an unfair constraint. I'd been backsliding into old habits: claiming to feel sick at mealtimes, frisbeeing my food at the walls; I'd pretty much given up altogether because recovery felt too hard.

Anyway, I'm glad I let myself be talked into going to that show – it was the gayest thing I'd ever seen in my life! I got to sit in the front row, within touching distance of this gorgeous, androgynous mezzo-soprano in a cerise spangled zoot suit who played Dorian. I was absolutely mesmerised, especially when he delivered a pitch-perfect jazz blues solo about how he was just a lonely, misunderstood youth, who cared way too much about what other people thought.

I knew then I had to get well; but I also knew that enrolling in a drama school six miles from my hometown was completely wrong for me: I had to get as far away as possible from my old life and the people in it; because if I didn't, I would never embrace who I truly was.

* * *

When I returned from the theatre, Kate was standing outside the nurses' station chewing bubble gum and listening to her Walkman.

"What took yous so long?" she shrilled, pulling off her earphones. "I've been back nearly an hour and I'm bored out my bloody skull."

"You're back?"

"Aye," she grinned, "that's what I said, ya nutcase."

* * *

It was June, 1990, when I finally got out. The exams had been and gone, so I didn't have to return to school to face Hannah or my other classmates – in fact, I never saw Hannah Jeffery for another seventeen years, which was something I always deeply regretted.

I had three Highers though – enough to allow me to scrape through the initial UCAS application process. Auditions were trickier because I was still too ill to travel, but thanks to Sally the occupational therapist's letter of support I was permitted to submit a video, and I was subsequently offered a scholarship for a performance arts college in London. My mother was furious: she made it clear she would never support me pursuing a career in the arts; she thought Sally was irresponsible for encouraging me, and that I should be out looking for a 'proper job'. In the end, though, she didn't try to hold me back.

As for my overall recuperation, it was a slow and ongoing process, and there were missteps and setbacks, and days where I could barely get out of bed. I still attended out-patient appointments with the psychiatrist and the dietician right up until the week I left for my studies; and I still kept a food diary, and had regular weigh-ins. I didn't mind going back to the unit though, because by then I'd started to think maybe I wasn't such a terrible person – that being queer wasn't terrible. I was even making plans in my head to seek out other people like me once I was settled in the city; besides, I got to visit Kate who was still in there, and she became a lifelong pal.

CHAPTER 17

School's Not Out

BY HARVEY HUMPHREY
(THEY/THEM)

Harvey Humphrey is a queer, trans, non-binary disabled person living in Glasgow. Their work explores the everyday, relationships and bodies. They are an academic who turned their PhD into the *AS IS* play about trans and intersex activist relationships.

Content Warnings
Homophobia, Transphobia

Eric and Martin lived with Jenny
Jenny had a little doll called Anne
But it was all too much for Kenny
Enraged he told Dave who wrote a ban

Kenny, Davey and their Tory mates
Easily passed Section 28
A subordinate clause promotes hate
'Acceptability' shaped my fate

Just 2 weeks later look here's me
Kicking, crying, shitting and screaming
In a world that wasn't yet ready
Waving? Drowning? Maybe just dreaming

"Fucking Dyke" they would shout at play time
"Lezzer Gay" they would shout over lunch
"Dyke" again on the bus at home time
Coat hood pulled up tight, shoulders hunched

To avoid them throwing dog biscuits
Pedigree felt like my only chum
While they all excelled at ballistics
I'm dodging each and every crumb

Every day except Baker Days
Kenny's unknowing reprieve inset
other kids would torment assumed gays
they were taught no better – presumed threat

forced to sit girl – boy – girl – boy each year
left this girlboy with no space their own

trapped in this binary and in fear
no place to be at school or at home

It wasn't just us queer kids alone
LGBT teachers closeted
afraid of students and staff if truth be known
hiding their family called 'pretended'

In adulthood we emerged not straight
finding guidance and community
in shadows of section 28
queer teenadults now allowed to be.

CHAPTER 18

Scene Redacted

BY JAMES CORLEY
(HE/HIM)

James Corley is a playwright and filmmaker. His work includes *World's End*, and *The Scene*. James has been shortlisted for the Iris Prize for Best British Short.

Content Warnings
Homophobia

PREFACE

As a screenwriter in 2023 I'm lucky to write about gay lives without fear or censorship. I get to promote and celebrate it. But what would my work look like if the rules of section 28 applied to it?

Reading the scene through with the cuts and without creates two very different experiences. And for the lead character Nick, it's one of hope and one of despair.

INT. CLASSROOM, 1999 - DAY

Year 9 are waiting for the English teacher to arrive.

JAMIE is doing a provocative gesture to whoops from the class - apart from NICK.

> **JAMIE**
> You've gone quiet.

> **NICK**
> Have I?

> **JAMIE**
> You're going to be gay when you grow up.

Everyone laughs.

> **MIRANDA**
> He actually is!

NICK
(quietly)
No I'm not.

JAMIE
Then say it's wrong, go on - say it's wrong to be gay.

Beat.

MIRANDA
I think it's wrong.

The TEACHER walks in. She goes straight to the whiteboard, putting on the day's date.

TEACHER
What's that Miranda? What do you think is wrong?

Beat.

MIRANDA
Gay people, Ms.

*The **TEACHER** takes a second. She turns to the class.*

TEACHER

~~Being gay is not wrong. It's perfectly natu-~~
~~ral. Go back through history and tell me a time~~
~~where there wasn't diversity in sexuality - and~~
~~gender for that matter. It's part of our make-up~~
~~- and I hope some of you in this room will join~~
~~that brave and courageous minority who have~~
~~to deal with so much pain, especially from the~~
~~uninspired, narrow types, such as you both -~~
~~Jamie and Miranda - who seem intent in drag-~~
~~ging us back to a time that never was.~~

~~*JAMIE and MIRANDA go quiet.*~~ The **TEACHER** circles the date
on the board - 9/9/99.

TEACHER (CONT'D)
Now if you could all notice today's date.

The class stare at it blankly. **NICK** *wants to put up his hand.*

TEACHER (CONT'D)

Well, it won't ever be that again. ~~So as we inch closer to the new millennium, let's try to go in with our hearts and minds open, yes? Because whether I like it or not it's you all - you - that are the future.~~

Murmurs of "yes, Ms", as the class write the date in their books. ~~*NICK stays staring at the date, transfixed, before catching the TEACHER's eye, who looks at him with clear warmth and understanding.*~~

~~*He feels like it could be ok.*~~

CHAPTER 19

Troubles

BY JAIME STARR
(THEY/THEM)

Jaime Starr is a non-binary, queer, disabled, Irish, Jewish anarchist fairy. Jaime does community education and sensitivity reading. Their poetry is published in *Queer Icons: A Queer Bodies Anthology*, and *A Passover Anthology*.

Content Warnings
Sectarianism, Bullying, Homophobia, Transphobia, Sexual Violence, Suicidal Thoughts

The accepted narrative is that growing up in Northern Ireland during the Troubles there was always an "us" and a "them". If you were to believe the news, every last person born and raised in Northern Ireland knew their place in a rigid hierarchy and stuck to it like glue — never mingling, never transgressing.

It's true that from cradle to grave, thanks to schools and neighbourhoods being segregated along Catholic/Protestant lines, there are some who rarely speak to "them 'uns" from the other side of the peace wall. If your entire community structure is set up to facilitate such a divide, to ensure the children you play with at school, the sports clubs you attend, and the pubs you go to as adults are almost exclusively populated by people of the same background as you then why would you seek an alternative? But there have always (and will always be) those of us who defy these proscribed boundaries. We are both, we are neither, we slip back and forth across porous borders between identities. We have no interest in fitting — and we are everywhere.

Born in the early 1990s, I am what they call a 'ceasefire baby' who experienced most of their childhood after the first set of ceasefires in the mid '90s, the Good Friday Agreement in '97, the return of devolution (local government) and all the other hopeful symbols of change and advances in equality that came with them. Change was the name of the game — in many ways. There were even cross-community schemes set up to facilitate links between Catholic and Protestant children (the one portrayed in *Derry Girls* is hilariously accurate to my experience of them).

But despite all this change, those of us still in school were still squashed under the homophobic legislation from Westminster which banned any discussion about sexuality or gender diversity. In a province that didn't decriminalise homosexuality at all until 1982 (15 years after the law changed in England and Wales, and only successfully changed at all thanks to the European Court of Human Rights intervening), it makes sense that revoking Section 28 wasn't high on the agenda even for most of the adult LGBTQIA+ activists in the province. There were so many other forms of discrimination to address, after all, in a country where one of the four prominent political parties was headed by Ian Paisley Senior — a man responsible for the campaign slogan "Ulster Says No To Sodomy", and later our First Minister.

I didn't hear the words 'Section 28' until I was an adult — I had no awareness of the laws and regulations that governed this aspect of our lives, only their effects on myself and friends who were ground down beneath them. The first time I butted up against Section 28, I was eleven years old. I hadn't a word for what I was yet, but there were other girls at Victoria College who had plenty of words for what I was. A bigger child with no interest in shaving my developing body hair and no real need to wear a bra yet, the lack of conformity of my body to the high femme standards of the popular girls led them to suspect me of deviance. 'Dyke' was one of their two preferred terms — that and 'gay boy' (which was interestingly far closer to who I have turned out to be, though they weren't using it to affirm my gender, of course!). The bullying utterly baffled me — I had to ask my mum what dyke meant, and when she asked where I had heard it, she went to the school straight away.

What she got was a discussion about how if I made more of an effort to fit in and be less "obvious" I wouldn't get bullied anymore. What I got in response to my mum's intervention was a one-on-one meeting with my head of year — Mrs E was in her late forties and proud of her work as a church elder. The understanding I had was that her place in the church meant she was kind and trustworthy. So, when she began to grill me about whether I had tried to force myself on the two girls who had locked me in a bathroom and threatened to beat me up if I kept changing in the changing room with the rest of my class before P.E., I was filled with nothing but shame. I came away from this meeting thinking this was the way that queer people interacted with each other, and had no resources at my disposal to correct that impression. I was so afraid that I was going to harm somebody that I kept to myself for the rest of the term, losing precious opportunities to establish the sorts of friendships that would sustain me against the bullies.

The next year I was in a better place. I was the head librarian of the junior campus, and had started to conform in some ways to the expected body standards that had singled me out the year before. I also had access to queer adults in the form of my mum's boss and his husband now, and though I cringe now at how blatantly obvious it must have been to them why I was volunteering for summer jobs walking their dogs and in their office, I had found that extremely comforting. While I still hadn't figured out my gender, I knew we were the same in some ways.

This extracurricular access to queerness saved my life. I broached the subject with the counsellor I had begun to see, and he helped me to figure myself out. I was more confident that I wasn't automatically a deviant predator, and began to allow myself to make friends. Being at a non-denominational school (a school with a set Protestant faith, but which accepted children from across the community) I ended up with two separate friend groups — a set of tomboy Catholic cousins, and a tight-knit collection of high femme Protestant friends from the Tiger Bay estate. I fit in comfortably with both groups — spitting and cursing as creatively as possible with Siobhan and Aoife one day, and letting Lara, Carly and Jenna practice makeup and eyebrow shaping on me the next.

The code-switching I did between these groups was good practice for masking my queerness throughout the rest of my school career too. But the one place I felt safest to be my whole self was in the library — my own little fiefdom with clear rules, orderly expectations and logical reasons for them all. Until one day, thanks to Section 28 it all came tumbling down. We were tasked by the head librarian (the staff member paid to train us, Mrs MR) with creating posters for a Shakespeare celebration — I was in my element. My new pack of glitter gel pens got the workout of its life. My mum rented me a three-hour documentary series about Shakespeare's life from the video store and half-way through, there it was — the nugget of information that would ruin me. Shakespeare wrote love sonnets to a man. I could barely breathe. I went looking for the sonnets, touching the pages with shaking fingers, feeling awake and alive with the possibilities they offered. Of course, it had to go on the poster — the people had a right to know, to feel as electrified as I did! It was a single line on a vibrant A3 poster. "Shakespeare wrote love poetry (sonnets) to both men and women." It earned me a lunchtime lecture from Mrs MR for "slandering the Bard".

Screaming at me in her office adjoining the library, with the door cracked for all to hear, she said I had accused him of something disgusting. When I pushed back, insisting it was true and that I had heard it in a documentary led by a historian, she sneered at me that if it was true, I would be able to prove it using books from the school library. As a teacher, she knew full well that there were no resources in the school library permitted to mention LGBTQIA+ topics, and weaponised this to punish me. I didn't know this at the time, but I did know she wasn't being fair, and resigned as junior head librarian the very next day. As an adult, I have had the pleasure of hosting Shakespeare scholars giving workshops on queerness in Shakespeare's texts and life for rapt audiences of all ages. Every time I do it, heals a little more of that enthusiastic twelve-year-old who shattered in the wake of an adult manipulating the law to punish their queerness.

Without the library to occupy me, I spent more time online during breaks, using the school computer lab to find myself the queer teens I couldn't access in person. Gay Youth UK's forums allowed me to talk to my peers for the first time. I was able to catch up on socialising appropriately for my age, with people my own age — chatting about the popular music and films of the day as well as puzzling out our identities together. As well as being queer, I figured out I was trans in my third year of secondary school (though I didn't have a word for being non-binary until much later), and began to express myself more authentically. I wore a makeshift binder to school under my uniform, and during book review projects in English class I began to bring my own novels and biographies of famous queer people.

I especially liked Eddie Izzard's biography at the time, as she had grown up on the street behind ours in Bangor, and I felt less alone for knowing another trans person had walked the streets I walked. But most noticeably, at the end of fourth year I shaved off my chest-length hair. This is the only time Section 28 worked in my favour. Despite this clearly being out of step with the strict, conservative and feminine uniform requirements, when I returned to school in September with barely a few millimetres of stubble on my head I wasn't challenged on it at all, entirely because the teachers were afraid to mention my transgressive haircut for fear it was a sign of the queerness they weren't allowed to acknowledge!

During forth year, my mum started taking me to London for a trans youth project called Sci:Dentity (a group that would later transform into Gendered Intelligence) where I met other trans people my own age. We bonded as we created art processing our understandings of our own identities, which we showcased at Central School of Speech and Drama in front of a packed audience. These weekend-long respites from enforced girlhood in my school life were a vital survival device – hearing the name I was experimenting with using and the pronouns that made my heart soar kept me alive until I was able to leave school on my 16th birthday, the day of my final GCSE exam. After I left school I was finally able to fully socially transition — first to a masculine, binary male presentation, though later at university as trans community terminology progressed I discovered new words that fit better still. Eventually I grew secure enough in my understanding of myself to adopt a more fey, non-binary bearded femme look and they/them pronouns, which is where I happily remain to this day.

But that greater clarity of identity was a few years off from the scorching hot summer I left school, a summer where sixteen days after my sixteenth birthday, my mum and I flew back out to my safe, trans-friendly nest, London. We were there to help carry the flag at London Pride along with other parents and trans teens. In those streets, packed with heaving crowds of strangers waving and cheering us on, I finally felt emancipated after years of being crushed by Section 28. After years of being forbidden from ever truly being myself at school, not even to the handful of friends I managed to retain despite their uncertainty around my unspoken differences, suddenly I was not only capable of breathing freely, I was being celebrated for it.

The fact that this happened the day after my first appointment with a private doctor who approved me for hormone therapy made it feel as if the entire ordeal of reaching that point was worth it. With a sixteen year old's typical self-centredness, I remember feeling as if for me, the Pride March was an affirmation and celebration of my survival, even if nobody else knew it. As we trailed towards Trafalgar Square, I thought of all the times I had been desperate enough to consider suicide.

I was suddenly staggeringly aware that this was likely true for many of the others present – people who I'd been forbidden from learning even existed, let alone were like me – as well as many who hadn't made it, some of them dying for the same lonely reasons as those which had pushed me towards oblivion myself. I made a wild promise to remain alive then, and vowed to never let myself be forced back into the lonely darkness that Section 28 and those who implemented it had imposed on my life. I thought and hoped that perhaps one day I'd be the beacon for another queer person – proof that we could survive and end up happy, the beacon that these crowds were for me.

They say you grow through what you go through — but personally, I believe that I'd have grown a lot more effectively and healthily if I'd been able to see myself reflected in the school curriculum. What a blessing it would have felt like to hear a teacher casually mention when studying Carol Ann Duffy's poetry that she is a lesbian; inclusive and non-judgemental relationship education, or any mentions of LGBTQIA+ History Month when February rolled around each year. How much would it have helped me to have been met with kindness and understanding by even a single adult in my school when my queerness made itself apparent, either through bullying or my interests and self-presentation?

I sometimes imagine what I would be like now if, instead of being treated like a threat and a predator and a problem in my first year, I had been told I wasn't alone and wasn't abnormal. Would I have become victim to the predators who preyed on me later in my teens if I hadn't been taught by Mrs E that this is what queerness is? Would I have been better able to seek help and support for that abuse if she hadn't closed that door for me? The number of times I danced on the edge of suicide in the choking silence of Section 28, with the words 'dyke' and 'he-she' from my bullies, and 'perversion' and 'disgusting' ringing in my ears from the librarian's lecture, are too numerous to count.

I've never regretted leaving, and though the school threatened that I'd never amount to anything without staying for A-levels, I went to an FE college and studied the Social Sciences, and then to university to study History and Jewish Studies as I'd always dreamed, focusing down into queer histories around the world. I am a published poet and author, I lead community spaces for other queer and trans Jews, I am studying for a Master's in Public Heritage to further the preservation of queer and trans history, and more importantly than any of my achievements, I am happy. Married for ten years, with friends and loved ones who know and see the whole of me and all my queer joy.

I survived. But I imagine how much more expansive my time and capacity for other things would have been if I hadn't been fighting to stay alive the whole time. How much further could I have gone? What unknown achievements did Section 28 and its enforcers rob me of? It's those unknowns — for myself and all the others who did and didn't survive Section 28 — that haunt me if I pause to think about them for too long.

CHAPTER 20

No

BY QUENBY HARLEY
(THEY/THEM)

Quenby Harley is an unapologeticlly fat, non-binary, and fabulous writer, performer and activist based in Leeds. Their ongoing project, Trans Joy, creates a space to focus on the positive side of trans experience.

Content Warnings
Homophobia, Transphobia

Aha no it doesn't stand for ally,
it actually means asexu-.
No, actually trans people have existed fo-.
No bi isn't the same as gree-.
No, that's not-.
Um no actual-.
No. No. No. NO.

I am done modulating my voice
Explaining every choice
I've made in the life I've lived
And I am done speaking for the privileged

I'm tired of being the punchline
Of people thinking it's fine
To make a joke about being trans or gay
And laugh at people who hear this every fucking day

I'm tired of people who talk about free speech
When that's the only human right they preach
The people who are fine reinforcing a prejudice
Which says I don't have the right to exist

Queer identity isn't a topic for debate
Pretending otherwise exposes a world of hate

A cascade of intolerance and disgust
Directed towards us

Because behind "protecting the kids"
There's an ideology that forbids
People who aren't cis and straight
Being spared from vehement hate

And when it feels like the world hates you
You know what you do?
You internalise that shit
You start to believe it

And it's not just words, I can't escape this
When I walk down the street I risk facing a fist
I choose between endless stares
And dysphoric despair

Calls for civility are a call for silence
A call to look away from a history of violence
Civility allowed people to ignore our plague
Using euphemisms and language vague

Cos homophobia
Is a phobia
An irrational fear
Of people who are queer

And if you're scared by me then so be it
Because whether or not you believe it
I'm scared too
I'm scared of you

I'm scared of becoming another sad statistic
And that's not just me being pessimistic
Our past and our existence is often a mystery
Because of silenced voices and erased history

So I will fight
For the right
For my voice to be heard
To not be treated as anomalous or absurd
I speak now to my queer sisters and brothers
Who've spent their lives being treated as others
Now is our chance for change
To not be seen as inhuman or strange

Today I say no to all this bullshit
Together, we can fight it

So be proud
Be fucking loud

CHAPTER 21

Don't Mention Your Mums!

BY BRYONY JOY KIRKPATRICK
(SHE/HER)

Bryony Joy Kirkpatrick is a 31 year old neurodiverse, bi/pansexual woman who has a dad and 2 mums. Occupational Therapy graduand with a background in applied drama. Lives in Southampton, widowed and currently a happily 'solo' cat mum.

Content Warnings
Homophobia

For me, Section 28 was defined by one thing in particular: being told in primary school not to talk about my family Being told not to talk about my parents. Not to say "I have two mums."

I particularly remember a PSHE lesson. I was in Year 4, and the teacher called me in in the morning before class and, in a very serious tone, told me:

"We're going to have this lesson on families, and I do not want you to mention that you have two mums, because a woman and a woman living together and having a relationship, or a man and a man, is wrong. So we don't want to spread that amongst the children, so please keep quiet about your family."

I remember feeling like my family was wrong, or shameful in some way. I knew that I didn't believe that, but I knew at that point, or I thought at that point in time that was what everyone else thought. So, I thought, if I wanted friends, then I had to be very secretive about my home life. For a kid, this is actually harder than people think or realise. Your home life is your whole world. Your parents are your everything, and that's what you constantly talk about – "I did this at the weekend, and we did that..."–it's quite a tricky thing, and being told that my family was wrong bred a lot of shame and low self-esteem.

When I started secondary school, I went in feeling the same. While I wasn't told explicitly by any teachers not to talk about my family, I went in knowing that that was the vibe, and silence was sort of expected. Back then it felt like, at school, everything bad, broken, or rubbish was called "gay". Things were either cool, or they were "gay". So there I was, once again feeling like my family was not going to be accepted, therefore I'd better not talk about it!

I was always a bit of a loner kid. I didn't fit in that well anyway, so I only had a couple of friends. They'd come round to my house occasionally and they knew about my family situation, but they didn't say anything. I remember going to school and the culture being very homophobic, so I was definitely not going to say anything.

At the end of Year 7, or early Year 8, one of my friends did mention it, just accidentally mentioned it to another girl, and it went like wildfire. It only got to me when I was very innocently walking from one class to another class. I was walking down the DT corridor of my school and all of a sudden this enormous girl, out of nowhere, pinned me up against the wall and was in my face, being, like, "Is it true that you're a lezzer?" and all this. And I was like, "No!" – "But is it true your mum is?" And I don't think I even said anything, I think I was too frightened. It was scary.

My best friend from primary school, still one of my close friends in my little group at secondary, was from a very strict Muslim family. She was not allowed to go around to anyone's house on the weekend or after school or anything like that. I never felt that I could tell her. because I distinctly remember a time several years prior her saying "it's really not OK for a woman and a woman, or a man and a man, to be in love, and if they do then they'll go to hell." So I remember thinking, "I'm never telling her!" but I really liked her and we used to play together, sit next to each other in lessons, and I just never said anything.

When news of my two mothers reached her, we were sat on the football pitch during a PE lesson. She turned to me and asked asked, "Is that true?" and I said, "Yeah, it is," and she said, "Well, I can't ever talk to you again!" We'd been besties since we were five, so that was quite hard. It was a little bit heart-breaking.

I did find a girl who was in my year, but not in any of my lessons – I was reading *Harry Potter* with a feather as a bookmark and she thought that was cool, so we became friends. She was part of a group of other misfits at the school, and when they found out they were all completely fine with it.

When I got to sixth form, things were completely different. I don't know what it is about the jump between secondary school and college, but it suddenly seemed to no longer be an issue. If anything, it made me more popular! I remember the first time someone was like, "Wait a minute, you have two mums?" and I was nervous saying yes, and they were like, "Cool!" And it became this really cool thing, "oh, you're really different!" which was very strange.

It was never a problem after that, but it definitely was something that weighed on me as a kid. Even having divorced parents, I remember, was a thing, let alone having two mums. I remember being quite small, maybe five or six, even before my mum was with her partner, and people judging my mum for being a single parent. And I told them, "Well, I do see my dad," but they thought that was terrible. People looked down on divorced women. I remember – well, I don't remember it, but my mum tells me - that my reception teacher came and did a home visit and gave her a lecture about me not having a male parental figure in the home. "Is there no *man* of the house?" My mum would take no shit, and cooly replied, "Well, I do have a lodger!"

Interestingly, people like teachers and older relatives would be really worried about me being gay. That was a whole thing for a long time. Older relatives, or older family friends, if they could ever get me on my own, they'd always make comments like… did I *know* it's men and women that get married? The amount of times I got asked, "Are you aware that women can't marry each other?" and I'd go, "Yes, I am aware, and I think they should!" Little things like that, you know, "girls wear dresses…"

I remember this one woman, she kept asking me, "Are you happy that your mum's given you a bobbed haircut? Don't you want to wear your hair long, and wear dresses?" And I was perfectly happy with whatever clothes they put on my body. I was a child, I didn't care.

I hope it's different now. I feel like it is.

CHAPTER 22

My Teacher Said "Gay"

BY JAMIE WAREHAM
(HE/HIM)

Jamie Wareham is the founder of QueerAF, an independent LGBTQIA+ publisher supporting queer creatives to build a media career. Journalist, award-winning digital media producer and Forbes Under 30 recipient, but ultimately a queer campaigner.

Content Warnings
Homophobia, Transphobia, Self-Harm, Bullying

Dialling the phone to my music teacher nearly 20 years on, I was nervous. Calling her by her first name was the first hurdle. The second was reliving that pivotal moment all those years ago. It didn't take long for us to embrace the subject. And even now, two decades later, she still wondered if she had gone too far. But trust me; my music teacher probably did more for me in those fleeting minutes, than anyone had for my whole time at school.

* * *

I went to secondary school when the insult "that's so gay" was at its peak. It was on the TV, and ablaze on the playground. Yet I arrived at 'big school' as the small, book-smart, weak kid who was desperate to blend in. My greatest fear was becoming what I'd already begun to work out - the insult everyone reached for, day in and day out.

My first step was to ditch the tap and jazz classes I went to on Saturday mornings. I loved them, but walking into those secondary school gates was walking through airport security gates that stripped you of all innocence. Big kids were here; so it was time to rip off the kiddy stuff and ditch it in the bin.

But more than that, I'd always known my enjoyment in dance and drama clubs was a tell from as early as primary school when we were taught it in class. In one PE lesson, we watched the opening scene of *West Side Story*. We were tasked to copy something we'd seen on screen. While everyone else trudged around the hall, clicking their fingers - I pranced. I remember the teachers pointing at me and whispering. It was one of the first times I realised I was different. I started clicking with everyone else.

Clearly, the lesson here was to blend in, to hide what I really was. I sought to get ahead and hide any lingering doubts the kids around me could pick up. I got a girlfriend. And as kind as she was, and as much as I liked her as a friend - she dumped me a few weeks in. In her defence, I barely even held her hand. But now I had that card in my hand, one of the first boys in the class to get a girlfriend. When I eventually came out many years later, dear Cait would tell me she knew way before I did.

It's a story many queer folks hear when they come out. Well, 'obviously'. Yet, it confirms our greatest fear that 'it' was on show all that time. That people knew our secret.

Like many LGBTQIA+ people who grew up with this hanging over our shoulders, I internalised that fear. I took on board all of that shame. I did everything to try not to be gay. I used what street smart I had and played the game. I found my 'group,' did my best to fit in, and projected my shame onto others.

I was lucky to make it through secondary school largely un-scathed. I can't say the same for a lesbian couple and the other gay guy who came out before me. They bore the brunt of a cruel homophobic culture that was in full rage in schools back then. The lesbian couple remained some of the kindest people I've known. Yet they navigated bullying in the dimly lit school corridors seemingly untarnished. Like they'd built an iron defence around them. Inside their tough exterior, I know it was a different story.

While the gay guy, well - he'd always been overtly camp. Unlike me, he embraced 'the stereotype' as his defence. He hid in plain sight. So when he came out, it was little surprise to anyone. Indeed, his fierce 'Regina George' approach that kept everyone at bay, and being friends with the popular girls, meant he could brush off the insults and bite back just as hard.

But there was one altercation that stuck with me. It likely held me back for years.

It's funny what you remember. Because I can't remember his name, but his face, I can still see that now. My crime was as innocent as getting to close to him on the unforgiving depths of the lower playground during winter PE. But it's vivid, how close he put his face against mine, the spit on my face dripping as he pulled away. The vile homophobic insult he threw as a warning shot after. It feels like it's happening now. It was brief but was a reminder that one toe out of line could mean being attacked for just being myself.

It just added to the growing pressure. The overwhelming urge to hide what I never wanted anyone to know, what I wouldn't accept. That I was different, that I fancied boys, and heaven forbid - I was gay.

When it became all too clear that the inevitable was unavoidable, no amount of 'telling myself off' for noticing handsome guys would make a difference. Trying to stamp out crushing on the cute lads wouldn't help. I turned to more challenging ways of coping. The kinds that leave scars.

Fortunately, I also had other outlets. Despite dumping dance, my creative flair wasn't entirely left untapped. I picked up the flute at secondary school and found great solace in the orchestra and becoming the school's music technology geek. The music block became a sanctum.

When the Year 11 exams came around, my depression was in full swing. I turned once again to the music department for solace. My music teacher was uncommonly kind. She picked up I was struggling long before I even knew myself. She reached out and offered safety and protection.

I could come and use the music practice rooms whenever I needed to. Which, at its worst, saw me in there during other classes, often in tears. The small cold rooms with broken and often boarded-up windows, the constant condensation, the drab, faded green walls - it was an unforgiving space.

The music department was in a stand-alone building apart from the rest of the school. Like me, it was separate from the rest but adjacent, trying to fit in with the rest of the school. This was where I chose to spend so much of my time.

One evening, after weeks of hiding away, my music teacher took an opportunity that would change me forever.

With everyone else gone home for the evening, she spied me alone in the corridor, looking at the times for my flute lesson that week. She jumped up from her desk and, without asking if I wanted to hear it - told me a simple story.

It was fleeting, almost tricky even to say it was a proper moment. But it was about her friend.

He'd had a tough time recently, a little like what I was going through. Though not *the same,* of course, she emphasised.

Except, he'd come to the other side of it. And the thing that had made him happier?

He'd come out as gay. Now he was living a happy life and was much better for it.

That was it. No embellishment, bare-bones in detail and not even time to paint a picture about her friend. Just a couple of simple sentences.

She just wanted to let me know that people come through the kinds of feelings - the depression - I was going through. That people get happier again.

I froze.

My face must have been a picture. I wanted it to say, "what's this got to do with me, miss?". Or "So what?".

But I think the tune my face was actually singing was:

How did you know this was what I was going through? Or even, is this made up just for me? How can someone else be going through the same thing as me? This can't be a real person!

Why would she tell me a story about her friend, no way, *surely* a teacher wouldn't tell me about *her friend.*

I dashed off without even making much comment to my music teacher. But my mind was racing. My feet couldn't move fast enough.

Scurrying off through the red brick tiles that our community school had on the quad, it finally happened. The first time I realised, or even considered that - being gay might be OK.

It's impossible to put into words this feeling. But it's like lifting a pair of sunglasses off to find the dreary gloom and storm clouds on the horizon you'd been watching for, well seemingly forever – actually, it turned out to be a sunny day after all.

You can't underestimate how much of a turning point this was for me. But I guess the fact that I came out a few weeks later tells you enough.

Given how low I was, it's fair to say - this moment not only saved me from all kinds of torment and torture I was putting myself through. It perhaps even *saved me.*

I started secondary school the year Section 28 was repealed. And so, less than five years before, my teacher lifted me from depression, self-harm, and suicidal thoughts with a quick story - what she did would have been illegal.

That bears repeating. Telling me a plain and, frankly, a rather dull story about her friend coming out and being happier for it – could have seen her lose her whole career.

Section 28 seems like a bizarre, weird law that even most queer folk don't understand. But when you stand it up to moments like these, the ones that liberate people from their internal horror - it's clear how cruel it was. How much it shrouded teachers from looking out for their students.

Speaking to my music teacher in the last few months, she really did wonder if she'd gone too far by telling me that story. I, of course, assured her otherwise.

But that lingering thought, even two decades later, shows what a hangover Section 28 has caused. Even now, that basic story could still be considered 'too much.'

And that's the trouble with the legislation. The law was so vague, so much so it was never actually used. But it left a generation of teachers afraid to talk about LGBTQIA+ people.

That means even now, kids will be taught by teachers who, thanks to this long-repealed law, are unsure whether they can, can't, should or shouldn't talk about our lives.

I can't help but think of the countless others who should, could and need to hear stories as my music teacher told me.

That story determined my life; it has fuelled my career in journalism and the activism I've done as an adult. The stories I tell today.

Every step I take now is about making sure no one feels as alone as I did – until I heard that story.

When I caught up with her, my music teacher also asked me if I had any happy memories from school.

I paused and realised that in fact - I do. After coming out, I made some of my fondest.

Like when some of the 'cool' lads asked me to comment on how attractive they were.

Then there was rugby practice where the lads joked and genuinely fought over who I would pick to 'mud wrestle' with me as a sign of how attractive they were (FYI, at best, it was yanking the lad opposite's arms out of a push-up and into the mud).

I even met my first boyfriend. He went to another school, but I could show friends grainy pictures of us on my sliding Sony Ericson W850. We even passed the classic teenage ritual of giving each other unsightly hickeys on our necks. Actually, after that steamy make-out session at the park, we went to buy matching Topman scarves. I didn't take it off for weeks, even after the marks had faded because it resembled something much more special. I finally had someone to share all of me with.

I've kept hold of that scarf all these years later, because it's a reminder that all of this made those last few months at school after I came out, dare I say it - enjoyable. Like I was a teenager – *finally*.

Section 28's legacy is harsh. But it's not in our past. Even now, confusing messages about what schools and teachers can or can't do around transgender pupils are creating a looming shadow again. They're coming from all angles, from the government, the press and even the equality watchdog - creating similar conditions, albeit by the back door, making teachers think twice again.

It's made this generation's 'Section 28' harder to fight. This time there isn't anything to repeal or one issue to unite around. Instead, young LGBTQIA+ kids are left with teachers caught in a malaise of rhetoric and a revolving door of policies. And yet, amid this misdirection, there is one clear takeaway.

Except, unlike the ever-changing policies, it's easy to implement. And it's a universal lesson, regardless of your profession. Because if you're ever left wondering whether finding your way to tell queer kids they're OK, then know this;

You're never taking it too far.

CHAPTER 23

Cheated of a Sound Start in Life

BY LEN LUKOWSKI
(HE/HIM)

Len Lukowski is a queer writer and performer based in Glasgow. He writes poetry, fiction, lyrics and memoir. His debut pamphlet *The Bare Thing* was published in 2022 by Broken Sleep Books. He won the 2018 Wasafiri Life Writing Prize.

Content Warnings
Homophobia, Transphobia

I was six years old when Section 28 was introduced and, like many kids of the time, I was completely unaware of it. From eleven I went to Catholic school, so it's unlikely LGBTQIA+ people would have been presented as positive or normal anyway. It wasn't until I started university that I really became aware of the bill. At university I got involved in student politics and joined campaigns for its repeal. Section 28 was abolished in 2003, I was twenty.

Because it was all I knew growing up, it's hard to put my experiences of Section 28, and the society that enabled it, into any sort of coherent context. It's not something you can easily explain if it's all you've known. I liken it to the time before indoor smoking was banned — up until that point I didn't notice the air in bars and cafes was thick with smoke. Had I been old enough in 1988 to engage with the news I may have been aware of gay people as spreaders of a deadly virus, predators, or the punchlines of a joke, but that would have been about it.

Some might ask, if you didn't know it was happening, what harm did it do? It wasn't like many schools were rushing to normalise LGBTQIA+ people by 1988 anyway. The 'offensive' literature that prompted Thatcher to unleash such bile into the world —a wholesome picture book showing two dads as loving parents to a young daughter— was very much the exception rather than the rule of the time. The damage Section 28 did was to stop any progress being made in education at all, fifteen years of stunted growth during which time great headway could have been made in queer kids learning they were OK. In straight people, some of whom will now have grown up to become homophobic and transphobic parents to LGBTQIA+ kids, learning queers were ok. It closed an avenue pivotal to childhood development, in which we might have learned to feel worthy of acceptance and love. Imagine the things that could have been prevented in those fifteen years and beyond: the queer bashings, the stigmatisation of AIDS patients, the self-harm, the suicides, silence around safe gay sex at a time when a virus was ravaging the population. The Act Up slogan 'Silence = Death' was all too real, Section 28 was an act of violence.

When I try to think of my time at school I hit a blank and painful wall. I think I knew I was queer from a young age, though I did not always have the words and tried my best to suppress that part of me. The first time I heard the word 'lesbian' was when it was thrown at me during regular bullying. I didn't identify as trans until I was an adult (it never seemed like an option, it was not discussed at all) but I was certainly gender non-conforming as a child and was frequently reminded of this with sniggering refrains of 'is that a boy or a girl?' Teachers generally didn't challenge homophobic bullying: if they did take action it was very much framed as 'don't imply someone is such a terrible thing', no attempt made to address the bigotry. Because being queer was presented as seedy and shameful, I felt incredibly guilty when I got my first crush on a girl. Though I never told her, I felt that even the existence of my feelings towards her was somehow a violation. I guess it's no surprise my Catholic school taught me sex should be between a man and a woman once they were married. My primary school was secular but I remember my teacher telling the class in the early nineties how values and morals had been going down the drain, but now, thankfully, the pendulum was swinging back the other way.

One of my first moments of awareness of queer politics came when the news showed footage of a demonstration to equalise the age of consent, I'll never forget my dad commenting, 'they just want younger and younger children'. In fairness to him, he had probably never met a single openly LGBTQIA+ person and was parroting the only 'education' the media was providing thirty years ago, but the comment still echoes in my head whenever I hear today's discourse in the UK and US about queers, and particularly trans people, 'grooming' children. I am sure the first I learnt about trans people would have been through trans women being made into the punch-line of a TV show or film. When I started to become more aware of my queerness I videotaped *Jerry Springer* episodes shown in the early hours of the morning because, trashy and exploitative as it was, it was the only time I would regularly see LGBTQIA+ people on TV.

There is not much sympathy in our culture for kids suffering daily abuse from their peers that, if inflicted on adults, would be regarded as horrific. Maybe it's because the perpetrators are other children. I'm nearly forty years old and still freak out whenever I hear people I don't know laughing, my automatic response is to assume it must be directed at me and there is worse cruelty to come. I've never really known how to talk about or deal with my experiences growing up, and often feel guilty or weak about feeling damaged by it because my experiences were the norm for most queer kids and some had it far worse, but perhaps that just shows how little we expect as queer people.

Around the late 90s/early 2000s I discovered a list of radical queer resources and zines online called Larry Bob's Queer Hotlist. Here I came across *Queers Read This/I Hate Straights*, a polemical anonymous leaflet distributed at Pride in New York in 1990. The pamphlet changed my feelings about myself overnight. I'd never read anything that angry by a queer person before; I didn't know we were allowed to feel like that. The pamphlet made me understand what straight people had been telling me about myself my entire life was wrong and it was OK, healthy even, to be enraged. Doubt-less such materials would have been called disgusting/brainwashing/

grooming at the time and probably by some elements of society today, but as a queer teenager it saved me. In reading the pamphlet, something in me snapped and the shame turned to rage. How fucked it was we were meant to coo over the marriage pictures of heterosexuals when we would likely get the shit kicked out of us for holding hands.

Section 28 didn't end in 2003. Before writing this essay I spoke to younger friends who were in school after the law was repealed, and it seems that for many, even a decade on, very little changed. Regardless of whether they went to a faith or secular school, their experiences could have been mine. At best, LGBTQIA+ people weren't talked about, or gay relationships were covered in an embarrassed hurry in sex ed lessons. At worst, teachers said things like, 'anal sex will always make you incontinent', and queer and trans pupils were ostracised, bullied to no response from teachers, or bullied by teachers. I asked some current or recent teachers what schools are like now around LGBTQIA+ education, and, whilst overall things seem vastly better, I've still heard some pretty shocking reports. More queer teachers are now able to be open about who they are, but what's really striking is how long it took, how some teachers still don't feel safe to be out in schools, how LGBTQIA+ inclusion is still very much a work in progress. Apart from some pioneering initiatives from a few brave teachers and campaigners who were the exception rather than the rule, Section 28 was effectively in force long after it was scrapped.

A friend who is an RSHP teacher in Scotland showed me recent curriculum material that teaches about queer and trans identities. She showed me a video about consent aimed at teenagers: the video shows queer couples as well as heterosexual ones without making any fuss over it. Slides for primary schools show families in all man-ifestations, including queer ones. I found myself wanting to well up on seeing the slides and videos. Contrary to what some believe, this isn't about brainwashing kids to be LGBTQIA+, it's undoing some of the horrific damage that comes from the straightjacket of heteronormativity, that hurts even cis straight people, who are still often scared of expressing parts of themselves lest they be seen as 'too gay'. I hope Thatcher's hell is wallpapered with LGBTQIA+ affirming slides.

Whilst LGBTQIA+ inclusion seems to be improving overall, now is not the time to be complacent. I was recently reading the excellent book *Bad Gays* by Ben Miller and Huw Lemmy, and what struck me was that attitudes to queer and trans people throughout history have never been a straight line towards greater acceptance - the value of your liberation may go down as well as up. It is hopeful that regressive institutions such as the Murdoch press are losing their influence on young people and Gen Z have a more positive attitude to LGBTQIA+ people than previous generations. Kids don't have to wait, like I did, until their late teens to find stuff on the internet or in popular culture to affirm their gender or sexuality. On the other hand, most power in the UK is firmly in the hands of those who would like to set the clock backwards. With reports the PM at the time of writing wants to review the Equality Act to inhibit trans rights, with the proliferation of exclusionary, supposedly feminist/ LGB groups whose only aim is attacking trans people, with the press running stigmatising articles on trans people every week, with discourse in the US and UK accusing trans and queer people of being 'groomers', there is much happening now that feels depressingly familiar.

I was cheated of a 'sound start in life' by Thatcher and those like her. I hope we can learn from the past, but I fear there are a lot of straight, cis people in positions of power who would prefer to use us as scapegoats for their own failures. We can't rely on increasingly right-wing politicians to advocate for us, nor for any marginalised people: we must come together, support one another and continue to fight.

CHAPTER 24

Baby Steps

BY OLIVER STARR
(HE/HIM)

Oliver Starr is a bisexual nerd. He keeps in touch with his inner child through live action roleplay, which is basically playing pretend with a few extra steps. He likes pirates, vampires and shiny lights and lives with the love of his life.

Content Warnings
Homophobia, Transphobia

PREFACE

I wrote this poem as someone who grew up under Section 28, but also as a nursery educator, working with children from birth to five years, and so much has changed since I was at school.

The sector-wide guidance on working with children, *Birth To Five Matters,* now says that "Attitudes toward gender and sexual orientation can limit children and create inequality" (Early Education, 2021). It gives advice on how to create an early years setting that is inclusive and welcoming of LGBTQIA+ children and families, and how best to provide both representation and acceptance in our nurseries with our resources as well as the language that we use.

When I first read about LGBTQIA+ inclusion in a highly influential, nationally recognised policy document I'm not ashamed to say that my queer heart wept with joy and hope. Prejudice is so much easier to learn than unlearn, and while the nursery environment is not a magic wand to wipe out homophobia, we are teaching children to accept themselves and others in a way that a few years ago would have seemed impossible.

The only time 'pretended family relationships' come up in early years these days is in relation to roleplay in the home area where yes, there can be as many mummies or daddies as the children want there to be!

BABY STEPS

They say that if you don't start ballet
by the time that you hit the age of four
learn the stretches,
and perfect the poses
grow in the music
like a plant grows in sunshine
the chances are
You're never going to be a dancer.

They say that if you want to learn a language
Speak it with fluency,
and conviction,
grasping grammar
as second nature,
so you can revel in its poetry
then it's best to learn
when you first start to talk.

I was queer in school.
Not queer as in fuck you,
But in the sense that I was fucked.

Fucked up
By the scars left.

I came out aged thirteen.

Not like a pride flag in the breeze

but like a McDonalds bag in the rain,
Less and less able to hold it together
After each new downpour.

Love was not love,
As they say now,
Not to the kids at my school.

I was eighteen
when section 28 was repealed.

I wondered if it had come
five years earlier
If it would have made a difference to
those hate and scorn filled kids?

Maybe it was already too late
the rot already taken root
too much for them to learn
Or to unlearn.

Would the ones who refused to change with me?

Still
refuse
to
change?

CHAPTER 25

Ask a Teacher

BY MANDY MCMILLAN
(SHE/HER)

Mandy MacMillan has been teaching Drama since 1991 in Glasgow schools. She lives in Glasgow with her wife and two children.

Content Warnings
Homophobia, Transphobia

I was in high school from 1980 to 1986. Section 28 hadn't been implemented at that point but there was no education then about LGBTQIA+ issues in my school. Name-calling, bullying and negativity about gay people were rife and teachers never addressed it. There were rumours about a couple of our teachers being gay, but no one admitted to anything. And especially not me, a young lesbian scared to tell her family and friends after years of listening to slurs and negative connotations of being gay.

It was all about the music in the 80s – lots of 'gender-bending' artists from Boy George to Annie Lennox; men wearing make-up (lots of kohl eyeliner), flouncy lace collars and flamboyant hairstyles - but this didn't lead to a more open-minded attitude when it came to sexuality, well certainly not in my wee North Lanarkshire town!

I became a teacher in 1991 at the age of twenty-two. I got a job teaching in a state comprehensive school in Glasgow. I had left my wee town, embraced my sexuality and wasn't going back in the closet. Section 28 had been introduced. I had fought against it during my time at University, helping organise a Gay Awareness Week and marching against it.

I vowed that I wasn't going to lie and not reveal my sexuality to my students if asked. I wasn't going to feel that shame. As a teacher we weren't allowed to 'promote homosexuality'. What did this actually mean? What was involved in 'promoting?' The dictionary definition is to 'support or actively encourage or further the progress of'. How could just talking about, or discussing, be seen as actively encouraging people to be gay? I wouldn't be actively encouraging them to be gay! I wasn't marketing 'being gay' and selling it to them. This way, I rationalised with myself, I could be myself and not risk losing my job. There was a very real and significant worry for LGBTQIA+ teachers that we could lose our jobs because of our sexuality.

When students asked me if I was gay, I had to be careful. I would never deny it but would answer 'Would it matter if I was?', 'Does that make me any less of a good teacher?' 'Does it matter who I go home to at the end of the day?'

As a student teacher in 1990, I worked with an English teacher who was teaching Edwin Morgan's love poems. The students responded well to the poetry and I asked the teacher if we were going to tell them that the poet wrote them to another man and that he was gay? I felt that it was relevant that they knew. A discussion followed with the class as to whether it mattered who the person was that the poem was written to and did that make a difference to them? 'Love is love' was the answer.

As a drama teacher, a lot of our curriculum and topics are chosen by the young people. They have to devise their own plays and they have freedom to do this. I cannot dictate the subjects they choose. I am there to guide, but ultimately at the end of the day, they pick the subject they are passionate about and devise their play. In the 90s I frequently had students choose subjects such as euthanasia, abortion, homosexuality, etc. It was very much 'issue-based' drama. The students would work on these plays and I remember one evening they were performing them to their parents and friends, a Deputy Head Teacher came and took notes from the back row.

The next morning I was summoned to his office. He was concerned about the topics. I reiterated that the pupils had chosen them and as this was part of their Higher Drama qualification I only had a very limited say in it. The school I taught in was a Catholic state school and I always made sure the pupils knew the Catholic line about these issues. I told them what the Catholic Church said, but if they decided to not agree with that, then what was I to do? I couldn't brainwash them. I also informed the Deputy that I was reading a play with students called *Brothers of Thunder* by Ann Marie Di Mambro about a young gay man, dying of AIDS, living with a Catholic priest.

He said he would like to read it. I duly gave him the book and said that it was being taught in other schools, and questioned: were we at the stage of banning books now? Were these children to get less of an education than others? Discussing and acknowledging that gay people exist is not 'promoting homosexuality'. He read the play and actually said it was a very good play and had some poignant points about forgiveness, reconciliation and the role of the church in the modern world.

Talking to students that I taught in the 90s/00s, as to whether having an out gay teacher made a difference to them, they said I made them just feel normal. For many of them I was the first person they came out to. They feel they were lucky as they know that was not the experience that many of their now gay peers had at their schools growing up.

Section 28 was being repealed in 2000 and I would travel to school seeing billboards Brian Souter, the campaigner to 'Keep the Clause', funded, with words like: 'They'll make your child role-play being gay!' I was a pregnant lesbian working in a Catholic school!

It was really difficult facing this level of homophobia in the media on a daily basis, and I know it had an impact on my students. The drama studio became that 'safe space' at lunchtimes. One student I know had been chased by a large group of pupils who sought to beat him with belts. The public debate and level of homophobia in the press had increased tensions and done a lot of damage.

When Section 28 was scrapped, nothing much changed. Teachers did not have the knowledge or confidence to support young LGBTQIA+ people. Perhaps the only thing that changed at first was the relief many LGBTQIA+ teachers felt that they would not lose their jobs if 'found out'!

I changed schools. I wanted to do more work for Equalities and Sexual Health within the curriculum, but was restricted under the Catholic education system. It took about another decade and the Equality Act 2010 being introduced before schools that I was involved in actively supported young LGBTQIA+ people throughout the school. The Act gave us the permission and the help to change things. LGBTQIA+ Youth Scotland worked with schools on their Charter Awards to help this. The 'Time for Inclusive Education', a remarkable campaign to get LGBTQIA+ Education embedded across the curriculum, was then enshrined in all Scottish schools. This has made a huge difference.

I ask students today about having out gay role models and teachers in school and it still makes a huge difference to them. They worry that teachers could be homophobic/transphobic/biphobic unless they are actively showing themselves as an ally within their classroom, e.g., with visible signs. They wonder if you can be 'out' at your work. They often don't have any adults who are LGBTQIA+ in their lives. They like it when they have a teacher who just 'gets it'. They can be themselves more and relax in your class and discuss the latest LGBTQIA+ character in a TV show.

I have now been teaching for thirty-one years. When I think back to the 90s when I taught thousands of young people who didn't have the support that we can provide now, I feel that they were robbed of something.

I know I did what little I could, but it wasn't enough. A generation of young people have been taught that they were an abomination, too shameful to mention, 'pretend families' and second-class citizens. Society owes a huge apology to those young people and we have to make sure we never go back to those times.

CHAPTER 26

Dam

BY QUEN TOOK
(THEY/THEM)

Quen Took is a trans and queer writer living in Manchester with two partners, four cats, and a spoilt Dachshund. A writer and scholar at the Manchester Writing School, they are working on their debut novel.

Content Warnings
Homophobia, Transphobia

They say I am dammed;
with mud-slung floors
and straw stuffed in my ribs.
Slurs become a slurry
of filth.

I use it to build walls.
I fall in love with every
brick hurled at my back.
I am gathering my harvest
unpicking grasses
and packing dirt down, down.

With every stone they throw at me,
I am building a dyke.

CHAPTER 27

Living Inside My Head

BY SARAH JONES
(SHE/HER)

Sarah grew up in the Southeast of England, realised she was gay around the time she started secondary school, and finally came out at the age of 19. She went to university in Manchester and has lived in lots of places around the UK and overseas. She has a partner of 25 years and they have two children together.

Content Warnings
Homophobia

PREFACE

This is the story of my childhood and teenage years under Thatcher. My memory of that time was that being gay was a shameful secret that you had to do your best to hide from people and, when Section 28 came into force in 1988, it added to that atmosphere of hostile silence. Needless to say, stopping people from talking to children about homosexuality didn't have the intended effect, though. I knew exactly who and what I was and no amount of fear and hatred and silencing was going to change that, even if I'd wanted to – which I didn't.

Section 28 came into force the year I turned 12, so it was the backdrop to my entire teenage years, but for a long time I didn't think it had had much impact on me at all. Unlike several of my friends, I never had a teacher refuse to talk to me about being gay or to support me when my parents threw me out (which didn't happen either). But that wasn't because I had unusually kind or brave teachers, it was because I never told anyone that I was gay.

I absorbed the messages all around me telling me that to be gay was shameful and disgusting and would make people hate you, and I kept my sexuality to myself. It is only more recently that I've come to realise that it was that silence that shaped me. I grew up in an atmosphere of isolation and fear that was, and remains, part of my sense of what it means to be gay.

I was about 10 when the vague and confusing feelings I'd always been aware of started to make sense and I clearly understood that I was attracted to other girls. I come from a family of readers and my dad, in particular, had a large collection of classic novels, which I was encouraged to pick up and read whenever I wanted. He had several of E.M. Forster's novels, and I had already read *A Passage to India* and *A Room with a View* and seen the Merchant Ivory film adaptations when *Maurice* was shown on the television. We had recently got a family video recorder and my dad decided to record the film.

I'm not sure if he knew what it was about – he didn't have the novel, so it's possible he hadn't read it – but in any case, he probably considered that if it was a Merchant Ivory production, based on an E. M. Forster novel, it must be okay. I don't actually remember the first time I watched the film, but I do remember immediately searching second-hand bookshops for a copy of the novel and reading it avidly during the summer holidays.

I remember being sat in my grandma's living room during a visit, waiting for everyone to get ready because we were going out for the day, reading and re-reading the scene when Maurice climbs up a drainpipe to the window of Clive's room and hears Clive calling out his name in his sleep.

I also remember the sense of excitement and joy at the discovery that it was possible for two men to love each other, and the confusion I felt for a few days (or maybe weeks?) until I decided that if that was possible for men, it must be possible for women too. By the time I returned to school that September, I knew I was gay; I just didn't have a word for it, and believed I had invented lesbianism and was the only gay woman in the world.

Although this revelation had a profound impact on me, on the outside, nothing changed. I didn't tell another person until I was 19, so my entire teenage years were spent in an odd split reality where what was happening all around me, and my relationships with my friends and family, were completely disconnected from what was going on in my head. In the environment that I grew up in, there was almost complete silence about homosexuality.

Nobody in my daily life ever talked about it. I don't remember it ever being mentioned at home or at school. I learnt about the mechanics of human reproduction in biology when I was about 13 or 14, and finally had a sex education lesson at school when I was 17 (too late for some!) but there was no mention of the possibility that we might be anything other than straight. It was clearly a shameful subject that was too shocking to be talked about and I absorbed that message.

In the wider world, homosexuality was a terrible, disgusting and frightening thing and my brief encounters with these views taught me that being gay was something to hide and that if anyone found out, they would hate me and never want to have anything to do with me again. News of the AIDS crisis had not fully penetrated the sheltered world in which I lived in the early 1980s, but I do remember the 'Don't Die of Ignorance' adverts and being frightened by them without having any clear understanding of what they were about. My grandad, who was an ardent supporter of Margaret Thatcher and a terrifying man, used to rant at the dinner table when we visited about the leftie gays on nearby Brighton council, who apparently refused to fund the maintenance of his local bowling green.

They were figures of hatred, alongside the 'stupid' young women who walked around in mini-skirts apparently asking to be raped, and the gay vicar whom the Church of England had foolishly placed in my grandad's parish and whom my grandad, as a church warden, hounded from his post. Nobody ever contradicted him and I remember being sat in that room, wishing the floor would swallow me up and feeling this odd mixture of fear that my secret would be discovered and relieved solidarity with these people who were like me.

I'm not sure if there was anything on television. My mum disapproved of TV, so I hardly watched any and did not find any gay-related television until my late teens. Books were my only source of information and, after *Maurice*, I can vividly remember the two other times I came across references to same-sex desire in books. The first was a paragraph in my GCSE biology text book.

I must have been 15 or 16 and I was sitting in a lab at school during a lesson. I was never any good at sciences and I was bored and flicking through the textbook while the teacher explained something that I wasn't really listening to. By this time, I knew the word 'homosexuality' and looked for it everywhere.

When I found it in the index to my biology book, I was briefly excited, hoping that I was about to learn something new to add to my limited picture of what it meant to be gay. But when I turned to the page, there was just a short paragraph, explaining that homosexuality was something that occasionally occurred between men in situations where they had no access to women, such as in prisons. It was clear that homosexuality was something disgusting that had no place in normal life among ordinary people – and that it had nothing to do with women.

The second reference was in a bible quotation book. My parents were both atheists, so my only family trips to church as a child were for the Christmas Eve carol service and for weddings and funerals. But I went to a Church of England school and, at some point in my teenage years, searching for some kind of emotional or spiritual outlet for the feelings I had inside, I decided I would become a Christian. I took myself off to my local church (which, looking back, was pretty brave of me as I was extremely shy and didn't know a single person there), sat quietly in the back through Sunday morning services every week and gradually made a small place for myself in this community.

There was a girl around my age in the choir who had long brown hair and a bit of an attitude, and I wanted to join the choir so I could get to know her better. I couldn't figure out how to make that happen, but after I had been going for a while, the vicar invited me to join a confirmation class he was starting.

When I found out this girl from the choir would be going too, I agreed. Ironically, getting confirmed was to bring my brief period as a Christian to an end. We were all confirmed on the same day by the Bishop, who had come specially to hold the service and, at the end, he gave us each a book of Bible quotations as a confirmation present.

When I got home, I carried out my usual search of the index for the word 'homosexuality' and found it! How I'd managed to get this far without realising what the Bible had to say on the subject of homosexuality, I don't know, but the brief quotes from Paul's letters to the Romans and elsewhere convinced me that I had to make a choice between being gay or being a Christian. I was old enough to realise that that wasn't really a choice and I never went to church again.

All through these years of silence, my real life was going on in my head. At 11, I left my local mixed primary school and went to an all-girls secondary school in a large town ten miles away. I loved it!

My total lack of interest in boys was masked, to some extent, by the fact that there were no boys to interact with even if anyone had wanted to, and (so long as I kept it to myself) I was free to fancy a succession of girls. Although I knew nothing would ever happen between us, I would try to get to know these girls, hanging around and smiling a lot, helping them with their homework and always being painfully aware of exactly where in the room they were and whether they were looking in my direction.

By the time I was in my second year, I had a best friend, Louise, and was part of a group of five girls who were all a bit different in various ways. We certainly weren't the cool people, but we also weren't total outcasts – looking back, I think we were probably the academic ones, although I'm not sure I realised that at the time. One of these girls, Anna, was cooler than the rest of us. Her parents had got divorced when she was younger and she lived with her mum and stepdad and two younger siblings. Her mum listened to Radio 1 and, when we went round, would chat about music that was in the charts and things that were happening in normal life, in a way that was totally unimaginable with my mum, who literally didn't even know who Madonna was.

I fell in love with Anna and spent several years trying to act like a normal friend when I was secretly jealous of anyone who got to sit next to her or talk to her. She was very pretty and had short hair in a pixie cut. I remember being sat behind her sometimes in lessons looking at the back of her head and wondering what it would feel like to stroke my fingers over the soft hair at the nape of her neck. I never did, of course, although we did, in the end, become very close friends and she was really supportive when I finally decided to come out at 19.

In the meantime, things at home were getting pretty difficult. My parents had always had a terrible marriage. My mum was almost permanently angry and would complain at my dad constantly, shrinking away from him if he ever came near her. My dad – who has always been a very mild-mannered person – accepted this without comment, and when I was younger I assumed that this was normal. When all my friends' parents started to get divorced (usually as a result of their dads having affairs and leaving their mums) I naively assumed that this wouldn't happen with my parents because I knew my dad would never leave my mum.

I was right about my dad, but underestimated my mum. In my early teenage years, she started having affairs with other men, taking me on holidays with her as cover so that she could meet up with them, and exchanging love letters which it was my job to collect from a sympathetic neighbour who allowed my mum to have them posted to her house. The secrecy and lies went on for several years, getting more and more complicated, before my mum finally announced that she was going to leave my dad and she and I moved into one house, while my brother went to live with my dad in another town ten miles away.

This whole experience made me feel even more isolated. My mum's behaviour didn't fit the pattern of other parents' divorces, and the secrets she involved me in cut me off from my blissfully ignorant brother even before we went to live in different houses. None of it was a good advert for heterosexuality, and I promised myself that even if I never found a woman I loved to make a life with, I would never settle for something I didn't want just to fit in with other people's expectations.

By the time my parents actually separated, I was 15 and beginning to make connections between my own feelings and the world around me. I started going into stationers and bookshops in search of anything gay and eventually found the feminist magazine, *Every Woman*, which included the occasional letter from a lesbian reader. I read Jeannette Winterson's *Oranges are Not the Only Fruit* and then *Written on the Body,* and even took *Written on the Body* into school when we were asked to read out a passage from our favourite books.

Nobody said anything when I read out a section about two women having an affair; there was just a slightly awkward, bemused silence before the teacher moved onto the next person, which only increased my feeling of screaming into a void. A year or two later, I came across Channel Four's *Out on Tuesday* and I used to set the video recorder to tape them late at night and then watch them in secret after school before my mum got home from work. The world they described seemed so distant from my reality that I don't think I quite believed it was true, but it gave me some hope. I decided that if I could just grow up and get away from home, I might be able to find a different life where it was possible to tell people who I was and maybe even find someone who felt the same way too.

In the meantime, it was the secret feelings I had which got me through. Looking back, I was pretty depressed. I remember lying in bed in the mornings fantasising about falling down the stairs so I wouldn't have to get up and go through another day. When I was about 15, I started smoking because I'd been told it killed you and, although I was too scared to kill myself there and then, smoking seemed a good insurance policy that I wouldn't have to keep going through this forever and could at least cut things short.

Despite all the fear and hatred around homosexuality, though, the fact that I loved other women seemed to keep me separate in a good way as well as a bad way. I hugged this special secret inside myself and it gave me a warm glow which shielded me from the awfulness around me. It felt like the one real and good thing in a world that was full of lies and nastiness. I fell in love with several girls during those years and even though I never told them, the possibility of seeing them helped me get up in the morning and the dream that one day I would find a girl who would love me back gave me hope.

Two big things happened during my sixth form years. Firstly, I fell in love with a girl called Farah, in my history class. She was tall and had long dark brown hair and called me 'sweetie', which I loved. I was completely obsessed with her and looked forward to history lessons so I could see her and hope that she might occasionally say something to me. The other thing that happened was that I went out with a boy. I can't really remember why, now. I think by this time, it was starting to be more noticeable that I didn't show any interest in boys and everyone around me was either getting boyfriends or talking about it.

I remember lots of time being spent before school and during the lunch break looking at teenage girls' magazines and reading ridiculous tips such as 'if you find yourself sleeping with a guy after a date, you should make sure you wake up before him in the morning and sneak into the bathroom to reapply your makeup so you'll still look attractive when he sees you'. All of this must have made me feel under pressure to show willing. I do also clearly remember spending some time as a teenager trying to resolve the problem of how I would be able to have a baby (which I desperately wanted to do) and be gay.

At one point I decided that I would have to carry on pretending to be straight until I'd slept with a guy and got myself pregnant, and then I would be able to come out as gay afterwards. Perhaps my decision to go out with a boy was part of this plan. Whatever it was, it didn't go very well. He was a nice enough boy and reminded me of my brother, which meant I was at least able to have a fairly relaxed conversation with him.

The physical side was less successful, however, as I really didn't want to kiss him and he must have sensed that something was wrong because, after a mere two weeks, he dumped me! I was oddly upset about this, perhaps because it was briefly a relief to have a relationship that actually existed in real life and other people were pleased about, but the experience also helped me to realise that I couldn't go on much longer keeping my real feelings bottled up inside.

I decided that I would come out as gay as soon as I left home to go to university. I chose a university in a city three hundred miles from where I grew up in the hope that this would be a different, and more gay-friendly world. The summer before I left was one of the longest and hardest of my life. It should have been obvious but I wasn't quite prepared for the shock of suddenly being cut off from everything – and everyone – that gave me a reason to get up in the morning. I'd got so used to living my life in my head that I forgot that it wasn't real to other people, and that relationships which meant so much to me didn't exist for them and there was no reason to carry them on after we left school.

By September, when it was time to set off to Manchester and start my new life, I knew I had to face up to things and be honest about who I really was. I only remember snatches of that terrifying first week of university. I had a room in a shared flat in student halls, and for the first few days my flatmates and I did everything together. I remember going round the freshers fair with them, trying to hang back so I could look at the stall for the LGB society without anyone noticing.

In the end, I think I must have gone back on my own and talked to those people, because I did somehow end up going to their meetings for a while. On the night of the first meeting, I realised I couldn't put it off any longer and told my flatmates where I was going and why. They were a little shocked, but much nicer than I had feared, and wished me luck.

The evening was not a success. The LGB crowd were a bit of an odd bunch and welcoming new members didn't seem to be part of their remit, so I spent most of the evening sitting on my own and wondering if being gay was going to be a disaster after all! I couldn't see myself being friends with any of these people, never mind wanting to go out with one of them and, in any case, lesbians seemed to be thin on the ground. Disappointed, but with no other obvious way of finding gay people, I kept going for a few more meetings, hoping that somehow things would improve. They didn't, but luck was on my side in a different way.

In their excitement at having met a real-life lesbian for the first time, my flatmates had got chatting to the girls in the flat opposite and discovered, to their amazement, that they had a lesbian flatmate too! It was decided that we should be introduced to each other and, as the lesbian opposite (Jenny) was a year older and definitely more self-possessed, she was sent to talk to me.

Jenny had short, spiky, bleach-blond hair and was extremely cool. I was very nervous, but reassured that she was quite friendly and more my idea of what a lesbian was meant to be like. She also had a girlfriend who worked in the trendiest gay bar in Manchester, and she offered to take me out on the scene and introduce me to her friends.

The first time out was a revelation. Although I was used to going to pubs, I had never been to a nightclub before and I had no idea what to expect. I have two memories of that night. The first is that I had turned up in jeans and a jumper (with no t-shirt underneath) and, ten minutes into dancing on a packed dancefloor, I was ready to pass out!

The second was that I had never seen so many gay people in my entire life. I was terrified and intimidated and had no idea what I was supposed to do, but the relief and excitement of being out and in a room full of women it was okay to be attracted to was almost overwhelming.

That place became my home.

CHAPTER 28

A Voice in the Silence

BY ELAINE SCATTERMOON
(SHE/HER)

Elaine Scattermoon is a journalist and (mostly retired) trans activist living in Glasgow with her small cat. She has written and talked about trans topics for several publications and media outlets as diverse as Metro, BBC World Service, New Socialist, and Glamour. Her hobbies include photography, poetry, and the Eurovision Song Contest.

Content Warnings
Homophobia, Transphobia

Section 28 was silencing. That's the main thing that I remember, in as much as you can remember the absence of something. It wasn't a complete avoidance of the topic, for we still had to deal with homophobia kicked around on the playground as casually as the football against the school wall, often by the same children. However, there was never anything said to balance this, nothing to cast the casual taunts of gayness into context, nothing to counter the idea that this was a fundamentally wrong way to be, something to be avoided, something shameful, something that you must keep to yourself lest you be cast away and disregarded. The taunts went unchallenged. It was silencing.

As a bisexual trans girl growing up in the 90s, there was never any hope for me, I may as well have been a Mojave cactus grown on the terrace of an ice hotel in northern Sweden, left to freeze under the cold stare of the aurora, never offered any warmth, never given enough light. There was no information to go off as to someone like myself, no map to my identity, and I was known as the isolated, lonely child who befriended more books and atlases than actual human beings. Nobody was going to explain to me, though even if they might have done, nobody probably could.

Being seen as gay in any way was a thing that was officially accepted but unofficially regarded as an aberration, a crime, and certainly not something that should ever been seen in someone still young enough to be in the Brownies - though she would have been forced to be in the Cubs instead. And being trans was a great unknown, a colossal perversion that was spoken of only in hushed tones on lurid late night programmes portraying vaginoplasty operations as if they were freak show circuses. Come one, come all, and witness the horrors of the sex change! Absolutely not something that should ever be so much as uttered within earshot of a child.

Even if that child were trans herself.

Tolerance was of course a major theme of my early schooling, before I went to Catholic secondary school and understanding the variations of humanity was put aside for ensuring a thorough knowledge of the sacraments and stations of the cross. In primary school, we took time to learn about other religions ('other' because you were of course expected to be at least some form of Christian) and about other cultures (even if through a conservative, quasi-nationalist lens).

Yet on matters of sexuality and gender, there was nothing. A conspicuous absence of it, though made less so when you didn't know what you should be looking for. We had crude sex education lessons but it was always taken for granted that the sex you were being oh-so-carefully taught about was going to be straight. Penis goes in Vagina, wear a condom, and that was about it, at least for the boys, and of course I was included in the boys, told to make sure I avoided making my future girlfriend pregnant too soon. For me, my sexuality and my gender a screaming nebula of scattered confusion, I was given no resources, no aid. For the gays, the bis, the trans kids, there was no tolerance. There was nothing.

I did know something was up. How could I not? While not every trans person has this experience, I was aware of the bugs in my existence from a very early stage. In Year 3, aged 8, I remember a girl in my class bringing in a magic wand she'd made with tin foil attached to a straw, and I tried making my own, solely to cast the one magic spell I longed for, the one that would make me a girl, and end the constant mismatch I was feeling.

I wrote stories about magic ways that 'boys' could become girls, and then ensured that they were never read by my teachers or parents lest they reveal my shameful secret that, despite the absence of information, I knew to be a sin. I had no idea that this was something that anyone else could ever feel, much less that transsexuality was known and well understood by that point. Perhaps in an ideal world I could have spoken to someone about it and the school could have reached out, but this wasn't an ideal world: this was a negative world, where instead of libraries we had fields of nothingness, and I searched in vain among the empty grass for some idea of what my deal could be. This went on for years, isolating me, nobody extending me much understanding, and nobody much caring. I made friends with worms on the playground because I had none among my classmates, who scorned me for my wrongness, teachers silent or worse.

In Year 4, I finally acquired a friend I could entrust with myself, a beautiful Muslim boy whose Middle Eastern family had recently moved into the area. We sat at the edge of the playground, far from the football against the wall, spinning stories with each other, discussing the world and ourselves and ourselves within that world. He too was isolated, rejected. He too suffered at the hands of our teacher, who delighted in the punishment of any nail that stuck out too far, something to be hammered back in, for their own good. After a few months, he suddenly disappeared, and I was alone again.

The teacher's husband, a supply teacher, disliked me just as much as his wife, and one day he lost his patience with my confused, earnest, curly-haired young self, and punched me across the face, sending me sprawling backwards into the little plastic chair I'd been sitting on previously. He lost his job, but the whole thing was kept quiet, and I was left isolated.

You make your own path when nobody has cleared one for you. Everyone you know is confidently walking along the road laid out for them, easily navigating every stair and every bend, and you, you are left to plunge on through the dense undergrowth, nettles stinging your knuckles, brambles catching at your legs, you caked in mud and out of breath, desperate for some respite from the journey.

You read every book in the library and yet none hold so much as a mirror to your own life, the only exceptions the brief, clinical definitions given in the encyclopedia about the mysterious half-humans known as the homosexuals, the transsexuals, the perverts, the deviants, the sexual, the adult, the forbidden. Surely that can't be you. Surely it must be you. You must be the one who is wrong. Every other plant around you is thriving, while your cactus is freezing, the frost killing its very roots. All the other kids are confident in their steps, you are tripping on vines as you clamber up a hillside tangle of weeds. Why can't you just be like them? What is wrong with you?

I'm sure the teachers knew. Some of them, at least. Even if I didn't say anything, even if I knew I must never say anything, must never betray my wrongness, they must have known. I was hardly a puzzle box except to my own lost self. Yet they couldn't say anything. Shouldn't say anything. Wouldn't say anything. Perhaps they hated me, perhaps they felt sorry and wished they could reach out, I never knew, but it's not like it made any difference when I was alone and everything was silencing.

It was understood that I was to be left alone and hopefully I would be fixed one day, do the decent thing and grow out of it, at least according to the politicians who claimed to know me and never did - figures I was only aware of through the news broadcasts I half-watched after my own programmes had finished. There were many thousands of other kids like me, but I never knew them. All I was aware of was that this was my own burden to carry, and I grew to thoroughly hate myself for it - for the wrongness of wanting desperately to be a girl more than I wanted to breathe, not to mention the wish to kiss 'other boys', run my fingers through their hair. Sins. And those who knew did nothing to help, not even to absolve them.

My primary school headmaster was different.

He was a gentle man. He was getting on in years, even back then, but had a kind face, wrinkled, with narrow-rimmed glasses and a patient, understanding smile. True, he told the same few stories over and over again in assemblies, especially in regard to his favourite hymn. "One more step along the world I go...". Everyone needing to find their own path, a lesson he'd mention in every final assembly of the school year. I got to know him well over my time in primary school, especially once I'd earned the ire of my teachers, and I was ordered to go to his office even when I'd only defended myself against a cruel jibe in class.

I grew to know that cold bench outside his office, uncomfortable and small, in a far corner of the hall - nobody else around except an occasional teacher who'd do their best to not look at you, and a ticking clock echoing in the empty space, to let you stew in the knowledge of your transgression before you were to face his judgement.

This particular time I'd been caught blowing kisses at some of the 'other' boys in the playground, and in the England of 1996, I may as well have stabbed another child for how that was treated. It hadn't been serious, but it's not like that remotely mattered in this context. It was a problem that was 'upsetting the children', and I was sent straight to the office, missing the start of the afternoon lesson - one

I'd been looking forward to - and was once more on that long, hard, wooden bench, listening to the clock mark the seconds until he was ready for me.

After an eternity, he opened the door and mentioned my name. I focused on my feet as the only things extant in the world and walked myself into his office, surprisingly small, and sat into the armchair he had for students, child-sized and extremely comfortable. I wondered what my parents would say - the punishment I would surely also face at home. Once more, I felt like I was being punished for something I was unable to help, but that had never made a difference before. This was, after all, my life, something I well understood even at the age of nine.

And this man, his rimmed glasses seemed to match the smile on his face, this man just gave me space, let me cry, and over some water, in a small plastic cup, told me:

That there was nothing wrong with what I did. That others might not get it.

That that was their problem. But that I should be careful anyway.

He didn't hug me, but it felt like the equivalent of a hug. It was a "I'm sorry the world is like this" talk delivered to someone whose teens were still years away. A personal version of his assembly speech, a reminder that I had a road for me after all, and I would go one more step along it, even while I felt like I was fighting through the undergrowth.

I always appreciated that, and held a spot of thankfulness in my heart, for how kindly he had always treated me; but I did not understand, until well over a decade later, the risk he had taken. Sure, he didn't explain gayness to me, and it's not as though transness even came up - I was far too careful to ever let on to anyone about that until well into secondary school - but I do recall how his kind words, his blaming of the world and not me, was exactly what he was not supposed to do then.

His role, as appointed by the politicians I never knew and who never knew me, was to push me away from That Sort Of Thing: not to tell me to effectively keep it under my hat until I found somewhere safe, years later, in a hopefully better world. Had the school governors, who were effectively a mafia council of middle-aged middle-class white suburban Tories who lamented the loss of Thatcher, found out about this, they would have had his job, his reputation, the school. And yet he still welcomed me. I feel sure if he had somehow known back then that I was a terrified girl thoroughly alienated from the world around her, he would have offered another cup of water, and given me another soft smile and a promise that things could get better, would get better, should get better, should be better.

Many years later, I saw a mention of his favourite hymn on Twitter, and I remembered my old headmaster, still recalling his smile despite the intervening decades. I tried looking him up to send him a heartfelt thank you for being the only one who gave me something in all the silence of my primary schooldays, but I was unable to learn anything about him other than that he retired a few years after I left for secondary school. He was getting on in years, I suppose, but still, I never got to send him that thank you, that tribute, from an older, far more confident me.

He was the exception. Things didn't improve for a long time after that. Alienated, alone, with a reputation for being both gay and insane, I was treated with ridicule, scorn, and suspicion by my peers. The abuse progressed to something physical, something sexual, absent of consent, on a school trip to the Lake District. It was an experience so traumatising that I ended up arranging to go to an entirely different school on the other side of my hometown, where I found one true friend to stand by me, a boy who would shield me from the bullies and whom I offered stories anew - a refuge at last.

I still recall hearing about the repeal of Section 28. At that point I was aware of its existence, aware of the void that had been created for me, the empty fields where my knowledge should have been, the silencing that ensured my self-hatred and my profound loneliness. It was a grey morning as the news came on over the radio, treated as a debate topic, abstract and philosophical, even while the very existence of me was argued about by politicians and media personalities without any involvement of me or my peers. I felt thoroughly powerless, in the back seat of the car, schoolbag on my lap, deeply distracted from the day's lessons ahead.

We turned off the busy dual carriageway and approached a roundabout in light traffic as a Tory explained to BBC Radio Five Live that LGBTQIA+ children simply didn't exist and that we were all created by malign influence from older peers, and I wanted to ask them how that could be true when nobody had been allowed to talk to us, nobody had been able to counter the bullying and the abuse with explanations or reassurances, nobody had been allowed to be kind rather than distant.

I understand the same politician would later claim that nobody knew any better at the time.

The legacy of Section 28 lived long after its death: its scent lingered in the classrooms and assembly halls. Teachers were now permitted to talk about gayness - maybe even transness, if they had any knowledge of it - and yet they did not. Gay teachers at my school remained firmly closeted to all but other staff, and homophobic and transphobic bullying was addressed solely as playing-field violence, devoid of the context it happened in, because nobody wanted to be the first to break the spirit of Section 28. Nobody seemed to know how. Even without the silencing, we still lived in the silence.

The only way I learned about transness was from the home-made websites of the earlier internet, Geocities sites with tiled backgrounds and flashing GIFs looping endlessly as American trans women talked about being TS and TG and about Genetic Girls and all that other terminology that we moved on from before the 2010s got underway. There was still nothing physically around me to explain who I was, that I wasn't insane and broken, that I wasn't simply warped by unrespected gayness but rather that I was one of many trans women throughout history. I only had the internet.

I'd later realise I was very unusual to get that knowledge at that age in that age, as I had to do a lot of my own research to even know what to be searching for. There was nobody and nothing to go off, not in the school social lessons, not in the library, nowhere about me but in those little niches of the web that my fellow trans women had begun to occupy. When I tried to transition a few years later, the school did their best to dissuade me, telling me they would not help me, and I was to not try it, even though they had no problem with it. No help was forthcoming on this front, even when I was the A-grade student the school used as a model pupil. They couldn't risk me being spoiled by transness or by gayness, they simply never wanted to take the risk.

The imprint of Section 28 remained.

Things did eventually improve, though only long after my own departure, long after I had left childhood behind and found different challenges, though it was, generally, not through the teachers. Yes, some would help, mostly quietly, a few kind words here and there, but like ripples along a river, the changes came from those of us upstream, each of us making our own path through that undergrowth leaving a trail for those behind us to follow. Slowly this became a new road, independent of any political debate on national radio, free of the indifference of the lasting traces of Section 28. Ironically, for all the newspaper front page scare stories of gayness (and transness) being passed from teenager to teenager like freshers' flu, we did help liberate one another, we did end up constructing our own refuges, we published our own libraries in the voids left by that hateful legislation. We had to do this for ourselves because nobody else was doing it for us.

Section 28 created a void, one left for us to fill, once we finally learned enough of the world around it to be able to piece together what had been missing - to tell ourselves and each other that there was, in fact, nothing wrong with us, but that the fault lay elsewhere. In radio politicians who thought if they left us nothing to go off, we would somehow repent and never grow into what they feared.

In a system that ensured that children could be hurt and not only would those doing the hurt not be stopped, but the pain wouldn't even be addressed. It was overlooked, the sound of our crying going deliberately unheard. In those who never had the courage to right the wrongs even after they legally could; in those who felt it best to play it safe for years into the future, ensuring that self-same isolation for those wondering why they were the way they were. It was a failed experiment. It was always going to be.

And yet despite all of that, quietly, there were still those who risked everything to help. Those who helped ensure that those of my generation were able to make it, so we could become the first link in a new chain, to build those roads for those walking after us, taking one more step along the world that otherwise cared little for them.

I think of my headmaster from primary school. I don't look back on my childhood with much fondness or nostalgia, but this was one man who went above and beyond to be a friend when a friend was needed. So I guess this is the tribute I was always going to write for him. I hope he got to be happy long after I left.

Section 28 may be now consigned to the past, and to the trauma and memory of those of us who lived through it. But the forces that caused it, the uncaring privileged few who wish to silence those they do not like by leaving them with nothing, but trying to ban their entire existence by proxy... those forces remain, and they continue to blight our world. They continue to leave wonderful people feeling deeply alone and wrong through their very existence.

For them, if you are ever able, always be that friend with a cup of water, a soft chair, and words of reassurance. And maybe then we can take one more step towards a future where nobody need fear a ticking clock, a hard bench, and averted gazes in the corner of the hall.

Be the one who speaks when everything else is silenced.

SUPPORT

While we have made every effort to include relevant and accurate content warnings at the start of each section, every reader will react to each of the chapters in this book differently. One book can never include the huge breadth of negative experiences that people encountered both before, during, and after the time of Section 28, and your experience during that time may vary from those shared here.

If you have been impacted in any way by the subject matter of this book, you may find the following UK-based support resources helpful:

The LGBTQ+ Foundation
Support Line: 0345 3 30 30 30
Email: helpline@lgbt.foundation

Switchboard LGBT
Support line: 0300 330 0630
Email: chris@switchboard.lgbt

Give Us A Shout
Text 'Switchboard' to 85258

MindLine Trans+
Support Line: 0300 330 5468

The Samaritans
Support Line: 116 123
Email: jo@samaritans.org

Gendered Intelligence
Call: 0330 3559 678
Email: supportline@genderedintelligence.co.uk
WhatsApp chat: 07592 650 496

If you'd like further resources to support LGBTQIA+ education in schools in the post-Section-28 era, more information and resources are available at www.lgbteducation.scot, www.tie.scot, www.diverseeducators.co.uk, or www.stonewall.org.uk.

Lastly, the editor would like to remind you that:

You are loved. You are valid. You are enough.

ACKNOWLEDGEMENTS

Some of our contributors would
like to make the following
acknowledgements:

ASH BROCKWELL

My chapter is dedicated to all my friends, teachers and mentors who helped me break the silence and live a more authentic and fulfilling life. In particular, thanks to Mrs Kinsella, Mrs Castino and Mrs Charisse for helping to kindle my love of writing, and to Rebecca D'Arcy, Sarah Sonraya Grace, Sandy Humby, Moriah Ama Hope, Jax Thomas, Adva Volk, Sharon Kernan, Jani Franck, and all the members of Sylvan Grove, Two:23, The Gathering Space, and MCC East London, for helping me navigate a spiritual path that doesn't deny my identity. A toast to the memory of Mrs Stokes, whose Typing room was always a safe space for the four queer misfits (we all got very good at touch-typing along the way, which was an added bonus!) and of my dear friend, mentor and Druid dad, Sandy 'Gillbride' Burnfield. And last but definitely not least, special thanks to Chrissie and Kestral for all your support, care and friendship on this '28' journey and beyond.

KESTRAL GAIAN

This is for the 80s kids who were queer 90s teenagers, finding ourselves through LiveJournal and random MSN chats, never sure if we were talking to another kid our age or someone much weirder. This is for S and R, who helped me through school, and for Ash, Alfonzo, Chris-Jae, George, and the countless other friends who encouraged me to embark on this project. This is for the family I love, who I kept too much of my life hidden from because of self-hate and fear. And, importantly, this is for every single incredible contributor to this book: thank you for trusting me with your stories, and thank you for your friendship.

DALTON HARRISON

I would like to thank Kestral and Ash for what they do in bringing the voices of the unheard together. They have put so much work into this and should be proud. I want to thank my mother in her memory. I hope I made her proud.

HARRIS EDDIE HILL

Thank you to all of my friends who stuck by me, even when it wasn't cool to do so, and even when you got bullied purely because of your association with me. I don't know how I would have got through such unchecked and relentless years of sanctioned queerphobia without you to love me as I am. I'm eternally grateful. I also want to acknowledge all of those people I never knew and will never meet, who fought for kids like me when no one else did. And to all of those queer kids who have followed, I hope you never have to deal with what we went through. I wish for you protected, unbridled and unashamed joy, and the chance to be who you are without limits.

LEN LUKOWSKI

I'd like to thank everyone who shared their stories with me about being queer pupils or teachers while I was writing the piece.

COLIN MACKAY

For Seb, thank you for helping me take my first few steps out of the closet; For my mum, who's first words after me coming out to her were "Thank God! I thought something was wrong!"; For Ash, my spouse, who has helped me unpack a lot, and I love with all my heart.

MANDY MCMILLAN

To all the LGBTQI+ pupils I have taught.

JOHN NAPLES-CAMPBELL

Ann Naples for teaching me how to stand up to hatred, believing in me and teaching me how to use my voice. Graeme Summers-

Campbell, my husband, who stands by me, loves me for me and enables me to continue to grow.

ELAINE SCATTERMOON

To Mr S, for giving me hope when all I knew was hopeless, to Daniel, for being my only friend when I needed one, and to a special woman in Bath who helped me write about past pain without me succuming to it.

GEORGE PARKER

With thanks to Phil, for holding space for me to discover who I am.

JAIME STARR

Jaime would like to express their eternal gratitude to their beloved husband Oliver Starr, who's love and support was fundamental to becoming the person they are today. They would also like to thank their loving parents, Lisa and Stephen, their brilliant sister Shannon for supporting them always, including on their chaotic gender exploration journey, even when it was tough, and their brother Nathan for always taking everything in his stride. Gratitude to Catherine MacNamara and Jay Stuart, the convenors of Sci:Dentity for giving them a space to discover themselves; and Duncan, Gavin, David and Vince for patiently putting up with Lisa's weird kid imprinting on them like a very queer duckling. Jaime's work is dedicated to the memory of their granny, Ellen Hughes, who always accepted and loved them unquestioningly, and who's easy acceptance of everyone is a perpetual inspiration to them.

OLIVER STARR

Oliver Starr would like to thank his wonderful and inspiring spouse and soulmate Jaime and his best friend Quen for their encouragement, kindness and cheerleading, and his mum for the unconditional love and casual acceptance that every child deserves but not enough receive.

QUEN TOOK

I would like to thank my wife, for being, as always, the first pair of eyes and ears on this poem. My husband, too, for bringing endless cups of coffee & drying endless tears. Finally, my poetry mentor & friend Andrew Macmillan, whose gentle encouragement brought me back to poetry.

JAMIE WAREHAM

To my uncommonly kind music teacher

CHRIS-JAE ANGEL

This is for all my black, brown and indigenous queer sibs who don't just hope for change, we stand up and demand it. We live through it. We exist despite it. For my trans+ fam who have nurtured, embraced and shared with me over the years, especially Kit, Shaira, Felix, Kestral, Iain, Alexandro, Cath, Jon. Y'all don't just glow, we get to glow together and no hate can break that strength. For Sam Mark Love, Curtis, Jock Mooney and Ed: You are what the definition of Allies should be. To Keyth, thank you for helping me share my voice, for believing in me and for fighting the same fight with a constant want of knowledge and understanding in your own growth. Melanie Joy Fontana - sisters since we were teens, regardless of the distance. To Paul, if you ever see this, thank you always, Come What May. Wayne, I Believe In You, ten out of ten Ana. And to Ad, thank you for leading an example as a powerful trans non-binary artist, person and friend and for showing me I had the ability to be the strong person I am now. I am forever grateful to you.

And ultimately, thank you to those of us who fought long before we did, those of us who weren't given the ability to make it through a world they were deserved of, and those of you reading this right now. You are worthy and you are valid. Regardless of what you were told and conditioned to believe: You are beautiful.

No story is too short, no life is too long and no existence is too much. Blessed be.

WITH THANKS

Reconnecting Rainbows Press would like to thank:

All of the incredible contributors to this book, and everyone mentioned in the stories who have been positive role models, mentors, and supporters over the years.

Alfonzo Sieveking and the staff at Common Press for providing a venue for meetings and events in the heart of London's East End.

Our launch tour venues: Common Press in London; The Old Fire Station in Oxford; Wharf Chambers in Leeds; Lovelock Cafe in Liverpool; The Pink Peacock in Glasgow; Lighthouse Bookshop in Edinburgh; Dyddiau Du in Cardiff; and anywhere else that has hosted or continues to host events dedicated to this book and the community it serves.

Chrissie Chevasutt and Megan Nightingale for ongoing emotional and practical support, including help with the launch events in Oxford and Cardiff respectively.

The team at QueerAF for spotlighting our call for contributors.

Queen Victoria Ortega, FLUX and the AIDS Health Foundation team for encouragement, positive energy, and financial assistance.

And finally coffee, through which all things are possible.

OTHER TITLES FROM RECONNECTING RAINBOWS PRESS

TransVerse, We Won't Be Erased!
Poems and Song Lyrics by Transgender and Non-Binary Writers
Edited by Ash Brockwell, 2019

TransVerse II, No Time For Silence:
Words of Survival, Resilience and Hope
Edited by Ash Brockwell, 2021

The Boy Behind The Wall:
Poems of Imprisonment and Freedom
Dalton Harrison, 2022

Counterweights - a poetry collection
Kestral Gaian, 2022

Hidden Lives - a young adult novel
Kestral Gaian, 2022

Emotional Literacy - a poetry collection
Ash Brockwell, 2022

Forthcoming:

TransVerse III, Transcendence:
Words of Faith, Love and Authenticity

Twisted Roots
A. G. Parker

TransVerse IV, The Wait Is Killing Us:
Trans and Non-Binary People Demand Healthcare Justice!

Songs of Remembering:
Singing Ourselves Back Together in a Broken World
Ash Brockwell

CPSIA information can be obtained
at www.ICGtesting.com
Printed in the USA
BVHW070508060223
657828BV00002B/204